Knit your own

Royal Wedding

Knit your own
Royal Wedding

FIONA GOBLE

Ivy Press

First published in the UK in 2011 by

Ivy Press
210 High Street
Lewes
East Sussex BN7 2NS
United Kingdom
www.ivypress.co.uk

British Library Cataloguing-in-Publication Data
A catalogue record for this book is available from the British Library

ISBN: 978-1-907332-79-1

This book was conceived, designed and produced by

Ivy Press
Creative Director *Peter Bridgewater*
Publisher *Sophie Collins*
Editorial Director *Tom Kitch*
Senior Designer *James Lawrence*
Designer *Clare Barber*
Photographer *Andrew Perris*
Illustrator *Ivan Hissey*
Wedding Planner *Hazel Songhurst*

Printed in the United Kingdom

Colour origination by Ivy Press Reprographics

10 9 8 7 6 5 4 3

Important!
Safety warning: knitted members of the royal family are not toys.
The figures have small, removable parts that are a choking hazard
and should be kept out of the reach of children.

Contents

A Royal Romance

When we heard that Prince William had finally asked his long-term girlfriend Kate Middleton to marry him, we didn't want knitting enthusiasts left out of the celebrations that were sweeping throughout the kingdom and the rest of the world.

The prince popped the question to Kate during a holiday in Kenya in the autumn of 2010. He presented his bride-to-be with a dazzling sapphire and diamond ring that had belonged to his late mother, Diana, Princess of Wales.

Tucked inside the pages of this book, you'll discover how to knit not just the couple in their wedding outfits, but also that wonderful blue dress Kate wore for the announcement.

There are patterns, too, for other members of the royal family. Of course, this includes the prince's grandmother, the Queen, who proclaimed that she was 'absolutely delighted' that the happy couple, who first met at the University of St Andrews in Scotland in 2001, were tying the knot.

After much speculation in the press, it was finally announced that Prince William and Kate would marry at Westminster Abbey, with the Archbishop of Canterbury, Dr Rowan Williams, performing the service. The Archbishop is here in his knitted form, complete with characteristic beard. You will also spot Prince William's father, Prince Charles (in his naval regalia), and his stepmother, Camilla. Prince Harry is also present and correct, in the distinctive outfit of the Blues and Royals of the Household Cavalry Regiment.

And if you want to knit your own guests, we've included patterns for a number of extra clothes and accessories which will fit all variations of the female and male dolls. All you need do is knit an extra male or female doll and choose the colour and style for the outfit. With a bit of practice, you can easily adapt the patterns to give your guests different complexions, hairstyles and expressions. And what's to stop you knitting a version of yourself to join in the celebrations?

It was also announced that after the marriage ceremony, the couple would take a carriage to the reception at Buckingham Palace, via London's historic Parliament Square, Whitehall, Horse Guards Parade and the Mall, and cheered on by thousands of people. To finish things off nicely, why not knit your own pair of footmen to escort the carriage? The whole royal family would finally appear together on the balcony at Buckingham Palace to greet the crowds of well-wishers, with the couple sealing the wonderful moment with a kiss. There is a special fold-out model of the balcony at the back of this book, allowing you to display your royal knits.

Above all, we hope that you will have a lot of fun knitting your own version of the royal wedding and that you will keep this book and your knitted royal family for years to come as a souvenir of Prince William's and Catherine's happy day.

*The happily knitted couple announced their engagement
to photographers from all around the world.*

Your Knitting Kit

Y̲ou don't need any special equipment to get started on your knitted royal wedding. If you're a seasoned knitter, you've almost certainly already got what you need. However, if you're a novice or an intermediate knitter, you may want to check through your workbox before you begin, just to make sure you have everything.

KNITTING NEEDLES

You will need ordinary knitting needles (sometimes called single-pointed needles) in three sizes to make all the projects in this book.

Because the projects are fairly small, it makes sense to choose shorter knitting needles than you would usually use for knitting garments. You will find that shorter needles are easier to work with. If they also have pointed ends, this should also make it easier to get into the stitches.

A PAIR OF SIZE 3 MM (US 2 OR 3) KNITTING NEEDLES

These are the basic needles that you will use to create the characters and most of their outfits. If you have a natural tendency to knit particularly tightly or particularly loosely, you may need slightly bigger or smaller needles, so check out the guide to tension (gauge) on page 11 before you buy.

A PAIR OF SIZE 2.75 MM (US 2) KNITTING NEEDLES

You will need these to knit the Archbishop's beard and the corgi's ears.

A PAIR OF SIZE 2.25 MM (US 1) KNITTING NEEDLES

You will need these to knit the female characters' shoes.

OTHER EQUIPMENT

In addition to knitting needles, you'll need some other equipment in your workbox to make your royal wedding.

A CROCHET HOOK

You will need a size 3.25 mm (US D-3) or similar size crochet hook to make crochet chains for some of the characters' hair and accessories.

A NEEDLE TO SEW YOUR WORK TOGETHER

Your characters and their clothes will be sewn together with the yarn you have chosen to knit them. You will need a needle with a sufficiently large eye for threading the yarn. It is helpful if the needle has a fairly blunt end so you do not risk splitting the yarn. Sometimes these needles are called 'yarn needles'. You can also use an ordinary tapestry or darning needle.

AN EMBROIDERY NEEDLE

Some of characters' features and a few of their clothes are embroidered with yarn. For this, you will need an embroidery needle with a sufficiently large eye for threading. While you may be able to use the same needle you used for sewing your work together, it is better to use a needle with a sharper point for the embroidery. This is because a sharp point makes it easier to get the needle in and out of your work.

AN ORDINARY SEWING NEEDLE

You will need this to sew the buttons, beads and sequins onto the characters' clothes and accessories.

A STITCH HOLDER, LARGE SAFETY PIN OR SPARE KNITTING NEEDLE

For some of the projects, you will need somewhere to hold spare stitches while you work on a particular section of your knitting. A stitch holder looks a bit like a cross between a knitting needle and a very large safety pin. Because the projects in this book are small, you may find a large safety pin will do the job just as well. Alternatively, you could leave your stitches on a spare knitting needle.

A COUPLE OF SMALL SAFETY PINS

These are useful for marking particular stitches in some of the projects instead of specially made row markers. Alternatively, you can simply use short lengths of normal thread, which you can tie around the stitches.

A ROW COUNTER

You can get several different types of row counters to help you keep track of the number of rows you have worked. If you think this will help you, it's worth investigating what is available. Many people find that a paper and pencil works just as well.

GLUE

You will probably find it easier to glue rather than sew some of the trimmings onto the clothes. Any PVA (white) glue that dries clear will be suitable for this.

FRAY-STOP GLUE

This is a special clear-drying liquid glue that can be used on the cut edges of ribbons and fabrics to stop them from fraying. It is available in most craft or haberdashery shops.

A RED COLOURING PENCIL

The cheeks of the characters are coloured by rubbing an ordinary red colouring pencil over the finished knitting. Don't be tempted to use felt pen or wax crayons to do this because the result will not be the same.

A WATER-SOLUBLE PEN

This looks and works like an ordinary felt pen but the ink disappears when it is sprayed or dabbed with water. You can buy these pens in most craft or haberdashery shops. You will find that a water-soluble pen is very useful to mark the position of the features on the characters before you stitch them. Before you use the pen, remember to test it on your knitting in an inconspicuous area to check that the ink will come out easily from the particular type of yarn you have used.

Making the Balcony

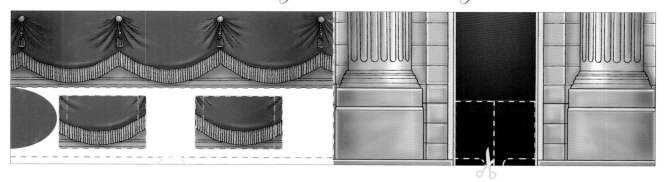

There's a cardboard balcony at the back of this book that you can construct to display your finished royal family.

To create the balcony, use a straight edge and a blunt knife to score along the blue dotted lines, then cut out the back panel along the yellow dotted line. Using a craft knife and a straight edge, carefully cut along the yellow dotted lines to separate the two side panels from the base of the front panel.

glue

glue

Cut along the edges of the two supports in the centre of the back panel and fold them back to stabilize the balcony. Use sticky tape or a small quantity of PVA (white) glue to stick together the front, side and back panels as shown.

Epic Yarns & Other Useful Things

Knitting the royal wedding is all about having fun and giving an individuality to each of the wedding characters. You do not have to stick rigidly to the colours and embellishments given in the patterns. For example, you may want to knit a turquoise dress, lime green coat and fuchsia hat for Camilla instead of the suggested colours. And instead of feathers, you may feel the urge to give her hat an enormous polka dot bow. So before rushing to buy new yarns, rummage through your stash or have a word with knitting friends. You could find something that is just perfect.

WOOLLY THOUGHTS

All the characters and most of their clothes and accessories are knitted in double knitting (DK) yarn. DK yarn can be made from 100% wool, 100% acrylic or a mix of wool and acrylic. DK yarns are also available in cotton and sometimes other fibres such as silk or bamboo. For these projects, we have used a combination of 100% wool yarns and wool mixes (wool mixed with acrylic or other fibres). The choice of yarns is yours but, where possible, avoid 100% acrylic and cotton yarns because they tend to be too flat and bulky and the results can be disappointing.

One or two projects require either 4-ply (fingering weight) yarn or a small amount of mohair yarn.

Some of the projects also use gold crochet yarn, which knits up well on 3 mm (US 2 or 3) knitting needles.

The shoes are knitted in silk rayon embroidery thread, and you will also need gold and silver metallic embroidery thread for some of the military decorations.

You will need to use ordinary sewing thread to sew the beads, sequins and fastenings onto the figures.

BAUBLES, BANGLES & BEADS

For the medals, jewellery and decorations, you will require a selection of sequins, ribbons, small fabric pieces, bows, beads, gems, tiny buttons and other trimmings. The specific items we have used are listed for each project. But if you feel like being exceptionally creative, why not raid your craft box and see what you can find to stamp your own mark on the royal wedding and its guests?

ALL STUFFED UP

The characters are stuffed with a 100% polyester filling that is specially made for stuffing handmade items such as toys. Check that the filling you buy is safe and conforms to safety standards. Do not overstuff your characters because this will make them look misshapen. Fluff up your stuffing before you use it and always remember to insert the filling a little at a time, easing the character into shape as you go.

TENSION (GAUGE)

The general knitting tension for the patterns in this book is 12 sts and 16 rows to a 4-cm (1½-inch) square over st st on 3 mm (US 2 or 3) knitting needles.

When you are knitting small items such as the royal wedding characters, your tension is not as important as when you are making clothes. But it is important that the knitted fabric you produce is fairly tight or your characters and their outfits may look misshapen and the stuffing will show through. If your tension is significantly looser, you should choose needles a size smaller. If your tension is significantly tighter, choose needles a size larger.

Abbreviations

K	knit
P	purl
st(s)	stitch(es)
st st	stocking stitch
beg	beginning
k2tog	knit the next 2 stitches together
p2tog	purl the next 2 stitches together
kwise	by knitting the stitch
pwise	by purling the stitch
inc1	increase one stitch (by knitting into the same stitch twice)
m1	make one stitch (by picking up the horizontal loop lying before the next stitch and knitting into the back of it)
s1	slip one (slip a stitch on to the right-hand needle without knitting it)
psso	pass slipped stitch over (pass the slipped stitch over the stitch just knitted)
ssk	slip, slip, knit (slip 2 stitches one at a time, then knit the 2 slipped stitches together)
rs	right side
ws	wrong side
yfwd	yarn forward (bring your yarn from the back of your work to the front)
rem	remaining
rep	repeat
cont	continue
g	gramme(s)
oz	ounce(s)
mm	millimetre(s)
cm	centimetre(s)
m	metre(s)
yd(s)	yard(s)

Knitty Gritty

The projects in this book are reasonably straightforward and do not involve any tricky techniques. The only stitches you have to know are the basic knit and purl. You will also need to know how to cast on and cast (bind) off, both on a knit and a purl row. Most of the items are knitted in stocking (stockinette) stitch (one row knit, one row purl) and some have some simple ribbing in them (alternate stripes of stocking and reverse stocking stitch formed by knitting one stitch and purling the next stitch). In order to shape your characters, you will have to be able to increase and decrease.

CASTING ON

You can cast on in several different ways but the method we suggest, which gives a nice firm edge, is called cable casting on and uses two needles.

1 First make a slip knot. Make a loop in your wool. Using your knitting needle, pull a second loop of yarn through this loop, then pull the knot quite tightly. This slip knot forms the first cast-on stitch.

2 To cast on more stitches, put the needle with the slip knot into your left hand. Hold the other needle in your right hand and insert the point of this needle into the slip knot and under the left needle. Wind the yarn from your ball of wool (not the yarn 'tail') around the tip of your right needle.

3 Now draw the yarn through your slip knot with the point of your right needle to form a loop.

4 Transfer the loop, which is your new stitch, onto your left needle. You will now have two stitches on your needle.

5 To make the next stitch, insert your right needle between the two stitches on the left needle and wind the yarn over the right needle from left to right.

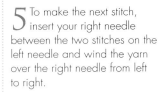

6 With your right needle, draw the yarn through the gap between the stitches to form a loop. Transfer the loop onto your left needle. You now have three cast-on stitches.

Repeat the last two steps until you have the required number of stitches on your needle.

THE KNIT STITCH

This is the most basic knitting stitch.

1 To make the first knit stitch, hold the needle with the cast-on stitches in your left hand. Insert the point of the right needle into the front of your first cast-on stitch.

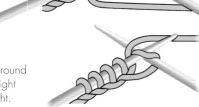

2 Wind your yarn around the point of your right needle, from left to right.

3 Now pull the yarn through the original stitch to form a loop on your right needle. This is the new stitch.

4 Now slip the original stitch off the left needle by gently pulling your right needle to the right. The new stitch will now be on your right needle.

Repeat these four steps until you have knitted all the stitches on your left needle. To knit the next row, turn your work, transferring the needle from your right hand to your left.

THE PURL STITCH

A purl stitch is like working a knit stitch backwards. Working alternate rows of knit and purl stitches creates a stitch known as stocking or stockinette stitch, which is the main stitch used in this book. The purl stitches are worked with the reverse side of your work facing you while the knit stitches are worked on the front.

1 To make your first purl stitch, hold the needle with the stitches in your left hand and make sure your yarn is at the front of your work. Insert your right needle through the front of the first stitch on your left needle, from right to left.

2 Wind your yarn around the needle from right to left.

3 With the tip of your right needle, pull the yarn through the original stitch to form a loop on your right needle. This is your new stitch.

4 Now slip the original stitch off the left needle by gently pulling your right needle to the right. Your new stitch will now be on your right needle.

Repeat these four steps until you have purled all the stitches on your left needle. To work the next row, transfer the needle from your right hand to your left.

CASTING (BINDING) OFF KNITWISE

The steps below describe how to cast (bind) off knitwise, which is the most usual way of casting off. They show you how to cast off on the right side of your work and also sometimes on the reverse. Try not to cast off too tightly or your work will look pulled.

1 First knit two stitches in the normal way. Then, using the point of your left needle, pick up the first stitch you knitted. Lift this stitch over the second stitch.

2 Knit the next stitch so you have two stitches on your needle again.

Repeat steps 1 and 2 until you have only one stitch left on your right needle. Cut the yarn, leaving a tail that you can use to sew your knitting together. Pull the tail through the last stitch by lifting up your right needle.

CASTING (BINDING) OFF PURLWISE

Sometimes you will need to cast (bind) off purlwise rather than knitwise, with the wrong side of your work facing you. Casting off purlwise is like casting off knitwise, except that you purl the stitches instead of knitting them.

1 First purl two stitches in the normal way. Then, using the point of your left needle, pick up the first stitch. Lift this stitch over the second stitch.

2 Purl the next stitch so that you have two stitches on your needle again.

Repeat steps 1 and 2 until you have only one stitch left on your right needle. You now need to cut the yarn, leaving a tail that you can use to sew your knitting together. Pull the tail through the last stitch by lifting up your right needle.

INCREASING M1

There are two main ways to increase the number of stitches. The usual way to make an additional stitch is to create a new stitch between two existing stitches. This type of increase is written as 'm1' which is short for 'make one stitch'.

1 At the point where you want the new stitch, pick up the horizontal loop that runs between the two stitches with your right needle.

2 Insert your left-hand needle from right to left through the front of the picked up strand, to transfer it to your left-hand needle. Now knit through the back of the stitch.

3 The increase is very neat and quite hard to spot within your knitting.

INCREASING INC1

Sometimes it is easier to increase the number of stitches in a different way. This type of increase is written as 'inc1' and it is important to remember that the 'inc1' refers to the extra stitch only. The 'second' stitch you knit is counted as an ordinary stitch. So the process explained below is actually 'inc1, K1' (increase one stitch, knit one stitch).

Start by knitting your stitch in the normal way. But instead of slipping the old stitch off the needle, knit through the back of it before sliding it off your needle.

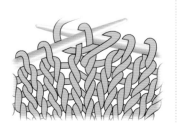

DECREASING K2TOG & P2TOG

There are a number of ways to reduce the number of stitches on your needle. The simplest way is to knit or purl two stitches together. In the patterns these types of decreases are written as 'k2tog' and 'p2tog' respectively.

K2TOG

Put your right needle through two stitches at once instead of one and knit in the usual way.

P2TOG

Put your right needle through two stitches at once instead of one and purl in the usual way.

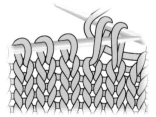

DECREASING SSK

Knitting or purling two stitches together produces a stitch that slopes to the right. However, when you are knitting something symmetrical you will usually want some stitches sloping to the left. This way of decreasing stitches is written as 'ssk', which is short for 'slip, slip, knit'.

First, slip one stitch and then the next stitch on to your right-hand needle, as if you were knitting them. Then insert the left-hand needle through the front loops of both these stitches and knit them in the usual way.

To Join Together

Learning how to join your pieces of knitting together evenly and tidily is crucial to the look of your work. Do it well and you'll be justifiably proud of your wedding cast. If you rush it, you'll be disappointed, so take your time. If it does go wrong – which always happens from time to time – undo it and redo it straightaway rather than waiting until the end.

THE JOINING STITCHES

There are two stitches that you will need to use to join your pieces together: mattress stitch and overcast stitch (also known as oversewing or whip stitch). The pieces are always joined using the yarn that the item was knitted in and a tapestry (or darning) needle.

MATTRESS STITCH

This is the recommended method for joining vertical edges such as the characters' arms. A slightly different form of the stitch is recommended for joining horizontal edges such as the tops of the characters' heads. Mattress stitch is not the quickest way of joining two pieces of knitting, but once you've got going, you will be delighted by its near-invisibility.

VERTICAL EDGES

To join two vertical edges with mattress stitch, place the two pieces side by side. Take the yarn under the running stitch between the first two stitches on one side, then under the corresponding running stitch between the first two stitches on the other side.

HORIZONTAL EDGES

To join two horizontal edges, take your needle under the two 'legs' of the last row of stitches on one piece of knitting, then under the two 'legs' of the corresponding stitch on the other piece of knitting.

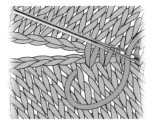

You can also use mattress stitch to join small pieces, such as the limbs, to the main body. This is a very neat join as the 'raw' edge of the top of the limb is completely concealed.

OVERCAST STITCH

This is the recommended way to join small pieces, or pieces with curved edges such as the characters' heads. It is also used to join small pieces, such as the ears, to the head.

To work this stitch, take the yarn from the front over the edge of your seam and out through the front again.

SEWING THE CHARACTERS TOGETHER

All the characters (with the exception of the corgi) are sewn together in the same way.

With the right sides of the head pieces together, oversew around the sides and chin. Turn the head the right-way out through the top and stuff. Seam the top of the head using mattress stitch.

Working from the lower edge, join one of the side seams, the top seam and then the other side seam using mattress stitch. Stuff the body and then close the lower edge using mattress stitch.

With the right sides of one leg and foot or shoe piece together, oversew the lower, back and top seams of the foot or shoes. Turn the piece the right way out and sew the back leg seam using mattress stitch. Stuff carefully. Repeat for the second leg.

With the right side of one arm piece together, oversew around the hand. Turn the arm the right-way out and sew the main seam using mattress stitch. Repeat for the second arm. Do not stuff the arms.

Join the arms to the top edges of the main body and the legs to the outer edges of the lower body using the technique described in the section on mattress stitch. Using the same technique, fasten the head to the body at the back and just under the chin. The face should overlap the top part of the body by about 1 cm (3/8 inch).

SEWING THE CLOTHES TOGETHER

The characters' clothes are sewn together using a combination of mattress stitch and overcast stitch.

JACKETS & COATS

All the jackets and coats are sewn together using the same techniques. First, sew the long seams that make up the sleeves, then insert the sleeves into the arm holes of the main piece and oversew them from the inside. Oversew any pockets in place. Finally, weave in and trim the loose yarn tails.

DRESSES & ROBES

The different dresses are all sewn together using similar techniques. First, sew the shoulder seams of the front and back together using mattress stitch (or oversew the shoulder seams of dresses with very thin shoulder straps). Join the side seams and, if the dress has sleeves, the sleeve seams using mattress stitch. Finally, weave in and trim the loose yarn tails.

TROUSERS

All the trousers are sewn together in the same way. First, using mattress stitch, join the back seam so that the lowest part of the seam is level with the crotch. Then join the two inside leg seams, again using mattress stitch. Lastly, weave in and trim the loose yarn tails.

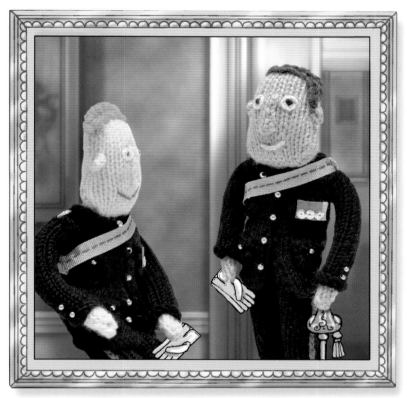

Prince Harry (left) and Prince William (right) in the uniforms of the Blues and Royals.

GETTING THE PERFECT FINISH

Once you have sewn your items together, your work is almost – but not quite – complete. To get the finished look on the characters' jackets, robes, coats and hats, you will need to soak the clothes in lukewarm water, shape them while they are still wet and then dry them flat. This technique is much better than trying to iron the garments, which will be fiddly and give them an unattractive flat look.

For items such as jackets and coats, you will also need to press down the lapels before drying them. For most of the hats, you will need to shape the top of the hat and press down and shape the brims. Generally speaking, the dresses and trousers do not need soaking and shaping in this way.

POSING THE FIGURES

The knitted characters are quite soft, so you may wish to stiffen them if you want to display them or put them in distinctive poses such as walking down the aisle or waving from the balcony. One method for stiffening them is to use PVC-covered garden wire. To stiffen their arms, cut a strip of wire approximately 12.5–14 cm (5–5½ inches) long. Hold the character's arms out so that there is a straight line from one hand to the other, then carefully thread the wire through the sleeves. To make the characters stand up on their own, first create a long loop of wire. Push the loop inside the back of the jacket or dress and run the ends of the wire down the back of the character's legs to make a base (for the male dolls, you can conceal the wire by running it inside their trouser legs).

Other Techniques

There are some other techniques that are useful to know before you start knitting your cast of wedding characters. Some of these are knitting tips and techniques, and others are sewing or embroidery techniques.

KNITTING, CROCHET & SEWING TECHNIQUES

These different techniques are essential for completing the projects in this book.

PICKING UP STITCHES ALONG A VERTICAL OR HORIZONTAL EDGE

For some of the projects, you will need to pick up stitches along a vertical, or cast-off or cast-on, edge of your knitting. This is usually referred to as 'pick up and knit'.

HORIZONTAL EDGES

If you are picking up stitches along a cast-off or cast-on edge, the process is similar but the number of stitches you need to pick up will always be the same as the number of loops along the cast-on edge.

VERTICAL EDGES

If you are picking up stitches along a vertical edge, with the right side of your work towards you, insert your needle between the running threads of the first two stitches. Wind your yarn around your needle and pull the new loop through. Sometimes you may find that you have more running threads than the number of stitches you need; if so, you will need to miss a running thread every few stitches.

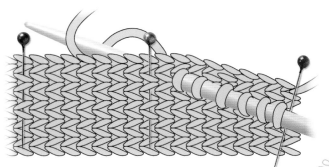

CROCHETING A CHAIN

Simple crochet chains are used for some of the characters' hair, to decorate some of the clothes and for some of the accessories.

1 To make a crochet chain, first form a slip knot on your crochet hook, as if you were starting to cast on for knitting. This is the first stitch in the chain. Holding the slip stitch on your hook, wind the yarn around the back of the hook and then bring it to the front. The yarn will now be caught in the slot of the crochet hook.

2 Pull the yarn through the loop already on your hook to make the second stitch in your crochet chain, as shown.

Continue in this way until the chain is the desired length.

CONCEALING & WEAVING-IN ENDS

When you have finished knitting your item and sewing it together, you will usually have some loose yarn tails that need weaving in.

On a character's body, simply take your needle into the body and outside at another point. Squash the body slightly and trim the yarn tail close to the surface. When the body springs back into shape, the tail will sink into the middle of the doll and be concealed.

After knitting a character's clothing, the easiest way to weave in the ends is to work a few small running stitches forwards and then backwards in the garment's seam. If your yarn is very smooth, take the needle between the threads of the yarn when you do this.

CONCEALING YOUR YARN WHEN SEWING FEATURES

When starting to sew a character's features, first make a knot at the end of your yarn. Then take your needle between stitches in an inconspicuous area and out at your starting point. Pull the yarn gently but firmly. The knot will be embedded somewhere in your item and the yarn will be secure.

Once you have finished the feature, take your needle back out through your work in an inconspicuous area. Work a couple of stitches, one on top of the other, in the running stitches between the knitted stitches (these will be slightly sunken). Then conceal the yarn in the manner described in the preceding section.

SEWING ON A SEQUIN

There are several methods used to sew on the sequins used to decorate the wedding cast's attire. They can be secured simply by making two or three stitches from the centre of the sequin to the outside. Alternatively, they can be secured with a French knot. But the most common method involves threading a small bead on top of the sequin then taking your thread back down through the hole in the sequin and securing it in an inconspicuous area either at the back or just underneath the sequin.

EMBROIDERY TECHNIQUES

There are a few basic embroidery stitches you will need to know to guarantee that your wedding characters look their absolute best.

STRAIGHT STITCH

This stitch is used for some of the characters' mouths and eyelashes. It is the simplest of all stitches – all that you do is take your thread out at one point and down at another point.

STAR STITCH

This stitch is used to decorate the Archbishop's robes. First work two straight stitches, one across the other, to form a simple, slightly flattened cross shape. Then work a vertical stitch down the middle of the cross you have just made.

FRENCH KNOT

This embroidery technique is used for the pupils of the characters' eyes. It is also used to fasten some of the sequins. To make sure the knot does not slip into the knitting, remember to bring your needle out and take it back down at a point between the strands of your yarn rather than in the gaps between stitches. Using a short length of yarn will also help make your work easier.

First, take the yarn out at your starting point. With your needle near the surface of your knitting, wind the yarn around the needle once (or twice if you prefer the pupils a little larger). Then take the tip of your needle back into your knitting, just to the side of your starting point.

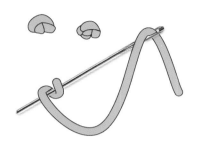

It is important you don't take your needle back into the exact starting point or your knot will slip right through. Continue pulling your needle through your work and slide the knot off the needle and onto your knitting.

CHAIN STITCH

This embroidery stitch is used for the irises of the eyes, for some characters' hair and teeth and for decorating some of the clothes.

First, take your needle out at the starting point for your stitch. Now take the needle back into your knitting, just next to your starting point, remembering not to pull too tightly so there is a little loop of yarn. Next, bring your needle back up through your knitting a stitch width along and catch in the loop. Pull your thread up gently until the stitch looks neat and firm, but be careful not to pull too tightly or your knitting will pucker.

You will need

FOR THE DOLL

25 g (1 oz), approx. 40 m/44 yds, of beige DK yarn

A small amount of black DK yarn

A small amount of mid-brown DK yarn

Very small amounts of cream and dark pink DK yarn

10–15 g (¼–½ oz) polyester toy stuffing

FOR THE CLOTHES

20 g (¾ oz), approx. 58 m/63 yds, of blue/grey DK yarn

A small amount of black DK yarn

A small amount of ochre DK yarn

A small amount of navy blue DK yarn

A short length of gold crochet yarn

Nine 3-mm (⅛-inch) gold beads for the buttons and securing some of the sequins

Two 5-mm (³⁄₁₆-inch) round gold sequins for the belt buckle and medal

An 8-mm (⁵⁄₁₆-inch) round gold sequin for the cap badge

A 10-mm (³⁄₈-inch) star-shaped silver sequin for the jacket medal

A 22-cm (8¾-inch) length of 12-mm (½-inch) royal blue ribbon for the sash

A small piece of striped ribbon for the medal

Use size 3 mm (US 2 or 3) knitting needles and a size 3.25 mm (US D-3) crochet hook

Prince William

THE GROOM

Handsome polo-playing Prince William is a flight lieutenant in the Royal Air Force and part of its search and rescue helicopter team. Shown here in a knitted version of his full uniform and the blue sash from the Order of the Garter, an elite group of British knights, he's well and truly prepared for his 'big day'.

DOLL

HEAD

The head is knitted from the forehead down to the chin.

Make 2 pieces

- Cast on 12 sts in beige.
- Work 12 rows in st st beg with a K row.
- Next row: K1, m1, K10, m1, K1. [14 sts]
- Work 7 rows in st st beg with a P row.
- Cast (bind) off.

EARS

Make 2

- Cast on 4 sts in beige.
- 1st row: (k2tog) twice. [2 sts]
- Next row: p2tog.
- Break yarn and pull it through rem st.

BODY

The body is knitted from the lower edge to the neck edge.

Make 2 pieces

- Cast on 14 sts in beige.
- Work 20 rows in st st beg with a K row.
- Next row: Cast (bind) off 1 st, K to end. [13 sts]
- Next row: Cast (bind) off 1 st pwise, P to end. [12 sts]
- Cast (bind) off.

LEGS & SHOES

The legs and shoes are knitted as one piece, from the sole of the shoe to the top of the thigh.

Make 2

- Cast on 28 sts in black.
- Work 4 rows in st st beg with a K row.
- Next row: K6, cast (bind) off 16 sts, K to end. [12 sts]
- Next row: P.
- Break yarn and join beige yarn.
- Work 24 rows in st st beg with a K row.
- Cast (bind) off loosely.

ARMS

The arms are knitted from the top of the shoulder to the tip of the hand.

Make 2

- Cast on 9 sts in beige.
- Work 24 rows in st st beg with a K row.
- Next row: K2, k2tog, K1, ssk, K2. [7 sts]
- Next row: p2tog, P3, p2tog. [5 sts]
- Cast (bind) off loosely.

MAKING UP

Stitch the doll together as described on page 16.

FEATURES

Embroider the nose in chain stitch using beige yarn. Using black yarn, embroider two French knots for the eyes. Using cream yarn, work a ring of chain stitch round each French knot. For the teeth, separate a short length of cream yarn lengthwise so you have two thinner lengths of yarn. Work a row of small chain stitches. For the lips, separate a short length of dark pink yarn lengthwise. Use one length to work two straight stitches, one next to the other, just above the teeth. Work two stitches in the same way just below the teeth. Use a red colouring pencil to colour the cheeks.

HAIR

For the hair, make two 8-cm (3¼-inch) crochet chains using mid-brown yarn. Arrange one round the front of the hair line (use the photograph on page 17 as a guide). Fold the other in half and stitch to the very top of the head.

TROUSERS

The trousers are knitted as one piece.

Make 1

- Cast on 14 sts for first leg in blue/grey.
- 1st row: K.
- Next row: P.
- K 2 rows.
- Work 24 rows in st st beg with a K row.
- Break yarn and leave sts on a spare needle or stitch holder.
- Work a second trouser leg exactly as the first but don't break yarn.
- Next row: K 14 sts from second trouser leg then knit across 14 sts from first trouser leg. [28 sts]
- Work 9 rows in st st beg with a P row.
- Next row: (K1, P1) to end.
- Rep last row once more.
- Cast (bind) off quite loosely, keeping to the K1, P1 pattern.

MAKING UP

Seam the trousers together as described on page 17.

JACKET

The two front sides and the back of the jacket are knitted as one piece, from the lower edge to the neck edge.

Make 1

- Cast on 36 sts in blue/grey.
- K 2 rows.
- Next and every ws row: K2, P to last 2 sts, K2.
- Work 10 rows in st st beg with a K row, remembering to K 2 sts at beg and end of every ws row.
- Next rs row: K9, k2tog, K14, k2tog, K9. [34 sts]
- Work 3 rows as set.
- Next rs row: K9, m1, K16, m1, K9. [36 sts]
- Work 5 rows as set.
- Next row: K11, turn and work on these sts only, leaving rem sts on needle.
- Next row: P to last 2 sts, K2.
- Next row: K.
- Rep these 2 rows once more.
- Next row: P to last 2 sts, K2.
- Next row: Cast (bind) off 2 sts, K to end. [9 sts]
- Break yarn and leave sts on needle.
- With rs facing, join yarn to rem 25 sts on needle.
- Next row: K14, turn and work on these sts only, leaving rem sts on needle.
- Work 6 rows in st st beg with a P row.
- Break yarn and leave sts on needle.
- With rs facing, join yarn to rem 11 sts.
- Next row: K.
- Next row: K2, P to end.
- Rep these 2 rows once more.
- Next row: K.
- Next row: Cast (bind) off 2 sts kwise, P to end. [9 sts]
- Break yarn and put all sts onto the needle holding the sts you have just knitted.
- Next row: K across 9 sts from first side piece, on back piece, (k2tog) 3 times, K2, (ssk) 3 times, K 9 sts from second side of jacket. [26 sts]
- K 2 rows.
- Cast (bind) off.

SLEEVES

Make 2

- Cast on 12 sts in blue/grey.
- K 2 rows.
- Next row: P.
- Break yarn and join black yarn, leaving long yarn 'tail'.
- Next row: K.
- Break yarn and join ochre yarn.
- Next row: P.
- Next row: Using black yarn 'tail', K.
- Rejoin blue/grey yarn.
- Work 19 rows in st st beg with a P row.
- Cast (bind) off loosely.

POCKETS

Make 4

- Cast on 6 sts in blue/grey.
- Work 5 rows in st st beg with a K row.
- Next row: K.
- Cast (bind) off.

BELT

Make 1

- Cast on 32 sts in navy blue.
- Cast (bind) off.

MAKING UP

Join the jacket pieces together as described on page 17.

DECORATION

Sew four small gold beads in place along the sideband of the left-hand front of William's jacket. Sew three small gold beads to the tops of the pockets (the left breast pocket does not have an added bead).

Sew the star-shaped silver sequin on the left-hand side of the jacket, securing it with a small gold bead. Place the ribbon over William's left shoulder and secure with a knot at his right hip. Sew a 5-mm (³/₁₆-inch) gold sequin on a small piece of striped ribbon for the medal. Sew or stick the

ribbon and sequin in place. Using gold crochet yarn, work two chain stitches at the top of the striped ribbon to represent the RAF emblem.

Using gold crochet yarn, run a line of running stitches round the length of the belt. Join the two short ends together and sew a 5-mm (³/₁₆-inch) gold sequin in the centre front of the belt for the buckle.

CAP

Prince William's cap is knitted in two main parts – the side band and the tip. The peak is knitted onto the side band once the two main parts of the cap have been stitched together.

SIDE BAND

- Cast on 22 sts in black.
- K 2 rows.
- Break yarn and join blue/grey yarn.
- Next row: P.
- Next row: K1, (m1, K1) to end. [43 sts]
- Work 2 rows in st st beg with a P row.
- Cast (bind) off kwise.

TIP

- Cast on 12 sts in blue/grey.
- 1st row: K1, inc1, K to last 2 sts, inc1, K1. [14 sts]
- Next row: P.
- Next row: K1, m1, K to last st, m1, K1. [16 sts]
- Next row: P.
- Rep last 2 rows twice more. [20 sts]
- Work 4 rows in st st beg with a K row.
- Next row: K1, k2tog, K to last 3 sts, ssk, K1. [18 sts]
- Next row: P.
- Rep last 2 rows twice more. [14 sts]
- Next row: K1, k2tog, K to last 3 sts, ssk, K1. [12 sts]
- Cast (bind) off kwise.

Join the short sides of the side band to form a circle and oversew the tip in place from the inside, so the rows of knitting lie across the width of the cap.

PEAK

- Using blue/grey yarn and with the rs of the cap facing you, pick up and knit 13 sts across the lower edge of the front of the rim, from one side to the other.
- Next row: P.
- Next row: K1, k2tog, K to last 3 sts, ssk, K1. [11 sts]
- Next row: P.
- Rep last 2 rows once more. [9 sts]
- Next row: K1, m1, K to last st, m1, K1. [11 sts]
- Next row: P.
- Next row: K1, m1, K to last st, m1, K1. [13 sts]
- Cast (bind) off kwise.

Fold the cast-off edge of the peak under. Oversew the sides of the peak together and the cast-off edge of the peak to the inside of the side band.

Sew the 8-mm (⁵/₁₆-inch) gold sequin on the front of the cap, securing it with a small gold bead.

Catherine Middleton

THE BRIDE

With her natural beauty, elegance and flair, Kate is destined to become one of the best-known style icons of our time. Dressed here in an elegant – albeit knitted – cream wedding robe and bejewelled silk shoes, not forgetting the beautiful tiara and sapphire engagement ring, she's just about ready to face the world's photographers.

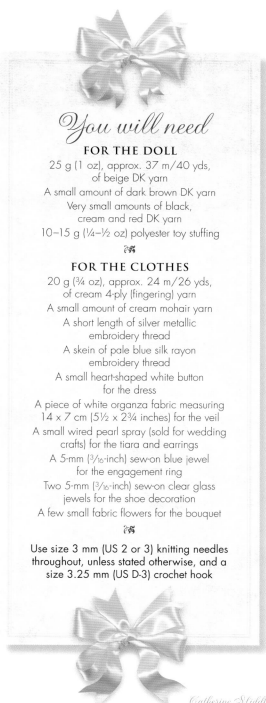

You will need

FOR THE DOLL
25 g (1 oz), approx. 37 m/40 yds, of beige DK yarn

A small amount of dark brown DK yarn

Very small amounts of black, cream and red DK yarn

10–15 g (¼–½ oz) polyester toy stuffing

FOR THE CLOTHES
20 g (¾ oz), approx. 24 m/26 yds, of cream 4-ply (fingering) yarn

A small amount of cream mohair yarn

A short length of silver metallic embroidery thread

A skein of pale blue silk rayon embroidery thread

A small heart-shaped white button for the dress

A piece of white organza fabric measuring 14 x 7 cm (5½ x 2¾ inches) for the veil

A small wired pearl spray (sold for wedding crafts) for the tiara and earrings

A 5-mm (³⁄₁₆-inch) sew-on blue jewel for the engagement ring

Two 5-mm (³⁄₁₆-inch) sew-on clear glass jewels for the shoe decoration

A few small fabric flowers for the bouquet

Use size 3 mm (US 2 or 3) knitting needles throughout, unless stated otherwise, and a size 3.25 mm (US D-3) crochet hook

DOLL

HEAD

The head is knitted from the base of the chin to the top of the forehead.

Make 2 pieces

- Cast on 6 sts in beige.
- 1st row: K1, inc1, K to last st, inc1, K1. [8 sts]
- Next row: P.
- Next row: K1, m1, K to last st, m1, K1. [10 sts]
- Next row: P.
- Rep last 2 rows twice more. [14 sts]
- Work 10 rows in st st beg with a K row.
- Next row: K2, k2tog, K6, ssk, K2. [12 sts]
- Next row: p2tog, P8, p2tog. [10 sts]
- Cast (bind) off.

BODY

The body is knitted from the lower edge to the neck edge.

Make 2 pieces

- Cast on 14 sts in beige.
- Work 8 rows in st st beg with a K row.
- Next row: K2, (k2tog) twice, K2, (ssk) twice, K2. [10 sts]
- Next row: P.
- Next row: K2, k2tog, K2, ssk, K2. [8 sts]
- Next row: P.
- Next row: K2, m1, K to last 2 sts, m1, K2. [10 sts]
- Next row: P.
- Rep last 2 rows twice more. [14 sts]
- Work 2 rows in st st beg with a K row.
- Next row: Cast (bind) off 1 st, K to end. [13 sts]
- Next row: Cast (bind) off 1 st pwise, P to end. [12 sts]
- Cast (bind) off.

LEGS

The legs are knitted as one piece, from the sole of the foot to the top of the thigh.

Make 2

- Cast on 20 sts in beige.
- Work 4 rows in st st beg with a K row.
- Next row: K5, cast (bind) off 10 sts, K to end. [10 sts]
- Work 19 rows in st st beg with a P row.
- Cast (bind) off loosely.

ARMS

The arms are knitted from the top of the shoulder to the tip of the hand.

Make 2

- Cast on 9 sts in beige.
- Work 24 rows in st st beg with a K row.
- Next row: K2, k2tog, K1, ssk, K2. [7 sts]
- Next row: p2tog, P3, p2tog. [5 sts]
- Cast (bind) off loosely.

MAKING UP

Stitch the doll together as described on page 16.

FEATURES

Embroider the nose in chain stitch using beige yarn. Using black yarn, embroider two French knots for the eyes. Using cream yarn, work a ring of chain stitch round each French knot. Separate a short length of black yarn lengthwise so you have two thinner lengths of yarn. Use the lengths to work a few straight stitches round each eye for the eyelashes. Use a separated length of red yarn to work two straight stitches for the mouth. Use a red colouring pencil to colour the cheeks.

HAIR

The hair is a formed from a series of crochet chain loops, apart from the wave at the front. Using dark brown yarn, make nine 20-cm (8-inch) crochet chains and one 15-cm (6-inch) crochet chain. Fold the nine longer chains in half and fasten them to the head using the tails at both ends. Weave the ends of the shorter chain into the chain. Join the chain to the front of the head at the centre.

DRESS

The front and back of the dress are identical.

Make 2 pieces

- Cast on 17 sts in cream mohair.
- K 2 rows.
- Next row: K1, (yfwd, k2tog) 8 times. [17 sts]
- Work 2 rows in st st beg with a P row.
- Next row: K.
- Break yarn and join cream DK yarn.
- Work 12 rows in st st beg with a K row.
- Next row: K2, k2tog, K9, ssk, K2. [15 sts]
- Work 7 rows in st st beg with a P row.
- Next row: K2, k2tog, K7, ssk, K2. [13 sts]
- Next row: P.
- Next row: K2, k2tog, K5, ssk, K2. [11 sts]
- Next row: P.
- K 2 rows.
- Work 2 rows in st st beg with a K row.
- Next row: K2, m1, K7, m1, K2. [13 sts]
- Next row: P.
- Next row: K2, m1, K9, m1, K2. [15 sts]
- Next row: P.
- Next row: K2, m1, K11, m1, K2. [17 sts]
- Mark beg and end of row just worked with a thread or safety pin
- Next row: P.
- Next row: K5, cast (bind) off 7 sts, K to end.
- Work on last 5 sts only, leaving other sts on needle.
- Next row: P4, K1.
- Next row: k2tog, K1, ssk. [3 sts]
- Next row: P2, K1
- Cast (bind) off.
- With ws facing, join yarn to neck edge of 5 sts rem on needle.
- Next row: K1, P4.
- Next row: k2tog, K1, ssk. [3 sts]
- Next row: K1, P2.
- Cast (bind) off.

Join the shoulder seams of the dress before knitting the sleeves.

- Using cream 4-ply (fingering) yarn and with rs facing you, pick up and knit 7 sts from marker to shoulder seam, then another 7 sts from shoulder seam to marker.
- Work 2 rows in st st beg with a P row.
- Next row: K.
- Cast (bind) off.
- Work the second sleeve in the same way.

MAKING UP

Seam the dress together as described on page 17. Secure the heart-shaped button to the front neck edge of the dress.

TIARA & VEIL

Create a circle from the pearl spray for the tiara. Seal the edges of the organza fabric with fray-stop glue and leave to dry. Using three strands of silver metallic embroidery thread, work a line of running stitch round the two short and one of the long edges. Using a single strand of the same embroidery thread, run a line of small running stitches along the other long edge, gather and fasten to the back of the tiara.

To finish, sew the tiara and veil on the head, sew two pearls from the spray for earrings and sew the blue jewel onto the doll's left hand.

SHOES

The shoes are knitted from the top edge to the bottom edge.
Make 2

- Using size 2.25 mm (US 1) needles, cast on 24 sts in pale blue silk rayon embroidery thread.
- Work 5 rows in st st beg with a K row.
- Next row: K.
- Cast (bind) off.

MAKING UP

Fold the strip widthways so that the right sides are together. Oversew the short edge and bottom seam (cast-off) edge. Oversew just under 1 cm (3/8 inch) of the top seam (cast-on) edge to form the toe section. Turn the shoe the right way out and secure the sew-on jewels in place.

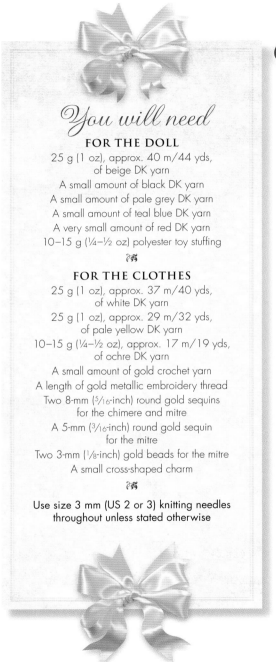

You will need

FOR THE DOLL

25 g (1 oz), approx. 40 m/44 yds,
of beige DK yarn

A small amount of black DK yarn

A small amount of pale grey DK yarn

A small amount of teal blue DK yarn

A very small amount of red DK yarn

10–15 g (¼–½ oz) polyester toy stuffing

FOR THE CLOTHES

25 g (1 oz), approx. 37 m/40 yds,
of white DK yarn

25 g (1 oz), approx. 29 m/32 yds,
of pale yellow DK yarn

10–15 g (¼–½ oz), approx. 17 m/19 yds,
of ochre DK yarn

A small amount of gold crochet yarn

A length of gold metallic embroidery thread

Two 8-mm (⁵⁄₁₆-inch) round gold sequins
for the chimere and mitre

A 5-mm (³⁄₁₆-inch) round gold sequin
for the mitre

Two 3-mm (¹⁄₈-inch) gold beads for the mitre

A small cross-shaped charm

Use size 3 mm (US 2 or 3) knitting needles
throughout unless stated otherwise

Rowan Williams
ARCHBISHOP OF CANTERBURY

Welsh-born Dr Rowan Williams, the Archbishop of Canterbury, is Bishop of the Diocese of Canterbury and leader of the Church of England. Shown here in knitted vestments, amply adorned with sparkling gold, he has something of a scholarly air. It's no surprise to learn that he is a poet and a superb linguist.

DOLL

HEAD

The head is knitted from the forehead down to the chin.

Make 2 pieces

- Cast on 12 sts in beige.
- Work 12 rows in st st beg with a K row.
- Next row: K1, m1, K10, m1, K1. [14 sts]
- Work 7 rows in st st beg with a P row.
- Cast (bind) off.

BODY

The body is knitted from the lower edge to the neck edge.

Make 2 pieces

- Cast on 14 sts in beige.
- Work 20 rows in st st beg with a K row.
- Next row: Cast (bind) off 1 st, K to end. [13 sts]
- Next row: Cast (bind) off 1 st pwise, P to end. [12 sts]
- Cast (bind) off.

LEGS & SHOES

The legs and shoes are knitted as one piece, from the sole of the shoe to the top of the thigh.

Make 2

- Cast on 28 sts in black.
- Work 4 rows in st st beg with a K row.
- Next row: K6, cast (bind) off 16 sts, K to end. [12 sts]
- Next row: P.
- Break yarn and join beige yarn.
- Work 24 rows in st st beg with a K row.
- Cast (bind) off loosely.

ARMS

The arms are knitted from the top of the shoulder to the tip of the hand.

Make 2

- Cast on 9 sts in beige.
- Work 24 rows in st st beg with a K row.

- Next row: K2, k2tog, K1, ssk, K2. [7 sts]
- Next row: p2tog, P3, p2tog. [5 sts]
- Cast (bind) off loosely.

MAKING UP

Stitch the doll together as described on page 16.

FEATURES

Embroider the nose in chain stitch using beige yarn. Using black yarn, embroider two French knots for the eyes. Separate a short length of red yarn lengthwise so you have two thinner lengths of yarn. Use one length to work two straight stitches in a V shape for the mouth.

SPECTACLES

Separate a short length of teal blue yarn lengthwise so you have two thinner lengths. Use these to work a row of chain stitches round the eyes to represent the spectacles.

HAIR

Sew a few loops of pale grey yarn to the side of the Archbishop's head for his hair.

BEARD & MOUSTACHE

- Using size 2.75 mm (US 2) needles, cast on 8 sts in pale grey.
- K 2 rows.
- Next row: k2tog, K4, k2tog. [6 sts]
- Next row: K.
- Next row: k2tog, K2, k2tog. [4 sts]
- Next row: K.
- Next row: (k2tog) twice. [2 sts]
- Cast (bind) off kwise.

Oversew the beard to the chin. Following the photograph opposite, work the sideburns, moustache and eyebrows in chain stitch using pale grey wool. Using an old toothbrush, dampen and then lightly brush the hair, eyebrows, moustache and beard to give them a slightly fuzzy look.

CASSOCK

Make 2 pieces

- Cast on 20 sts in white.
- Work 15 rows in st st beg with a P row.
- Next row: K2, ssk, K to last 4 sts, k2tog, K2. [18 sts]
- Work 9 rows in st st beg with a P row.
- Rep last 10 rows once more. [16 sts]
- Next row: K2, ssk, K to last 4 sts, k2tog, K2. [14 sts]
- Work 3 rows in st st beg with a P row.
- Mark beg and end of row just worked with a thread or safety pin.
- Work another 6 rows in st st beg with a K row.
- Next row: Cast (bind) off 3 sts, K to end. [11 sts]
- Next row: Cast (bind) off 3 sts pwise, P to end. [8 sts]
- Work 2 rows in st st beg with a K row.
- Next row: K1, m1, K6, m1, K1. [10 sts]
- Work 5 rows in st st beg with a P row.
- Cast (bind) off loosely.

Join the shoulder seams of the cassock before knitting the sleeves.

- Using white yarn and with rs facing you, pick up and K 8 sts from marker to shoulder seam and another 8 sts from shoulder seam to second marker. [16 sts]
- Work 11 rows in st st beg with a P row.
- Next row: K2, m1, K to last 2 sts, m1, K2. [18 sts]
- Work 3 rows in st st.
- Next row: K2, m1, K to last 2 sts, m1, K2. [20 sts]
- Next row: K.
- Work 3 rows in st st beg with a K row.
- Cast (bind) off kwise.
- Work the second sleeve in the same way.

MAKING UP

Join the side and sleeve seams of the cassock as described on page 17.

CHIMERE

The chimere, a sleeveless cloak, is knitted as one piece, from the neck edge downwards.

Make 1

- Cast on 24 sts in ochre.
- 1st row: P.
- Break yarn and join pale yellow yarn.
- Work 2 rows in st st beg with a K row.
- Next row: K6, m1, K12, m1, K6. [26 sts]
- Work 3 rows in st st beg with a P row.
- Next row: K6, m1, k1, m1, K12, m1, K1, m1, K6. [30 sts]
- Next row: P.
- Next row: K3, turn and work on these sts only, leaving other sts on needle.
- Next row: K1, P2.
- Next row: K.
- Next row: K1, P2.
- Rep last 2 rows three more times.
- Break yarn and leave sts just worked on stitch holder or large safety pin.
- With rs facing you, rejoin yarn to rem sts.
- Next row: K4, m1, K1, m1, K14, m1, K1, m1, K4, turn and work on these 28 sts only, leaving rem 3 sts on stitch holder or large safety pin.
- Next and every ws row: K1, P to last st, K1.
- Next rs row: K5, m1, K1, m1, K16, m1, K1, m1, K5. [32 sts]
- Work 3 rows as set.
- Next rs row: K6, m1, K1, m1, K18, m1, K1, m1, K6. [36 sts]
- Work 2 rows as set.
- Next row: K1, P to last st, K1.
- Break yarn. You can leave sts just worked on needle.
- With rs facing you, rejoin yarn to unworked group of 3 sts.
- Next row: K.
- Next row: P2, K1.
- Rep these 2 rows four times more.

- Break yarn and put all 42 sts back on one needle, ready to work a rs row.
- Work 30 rows in st st beg with a K row.
- Break yarn and join ochre yarn.
- Next row: K.
- Cast (bind) off kwise.
- Using ochre yarn and with rs facing you, pick up and K 42 sts up one front edge from the very bottom to the very top.
- K 3 rows.
- Cast (bind) off.
- Work the other front edge in the same way.

FASTENING

- Cast on 8 sts in ochre.
- K 4 rows.
- Cast (bind) off.

MAKING UP

Work a row of running stitch round the entire border of the garment using gold crochet yarn. Sew the fastening onto the reverse of both sides of both front edges of the chimere and sew an 8-mm (5/16-inch) sequin onto the cloak fastening. Work the stars using three strands of gold metallic embroidery thread.

MITRE

Make 2 pieces

- Cast on 12 sts in gold crochet yarn.
- K 2 rows.
- Next row: P.
- Break yarn and join ochre yarn.
- Work 2 rows in st st beg with a K row.
- Next row: K1, m1, K to last st, m1, K1. [14 sts]
- Work 3 rows in st st beg with a P row.
- Next row: K1, m1, K to last st, m1, K1. [16 sts]
- Next row: P.

- Next row: k2tog, K to last 2 sts, ssk. [14 sts]
- Next row: P.
- Rep last 2 rows three more times. [8 sts]
- Next row: k2tog, K to last 2 sts, ssk. [6 sts]
- Next row: p2tog, P2, p2tog. [4 sts]
- Next row: k2tog, ssk. [2 sts]
- Next row: p2tog, break yarn and pull yarn tail through rem st.

MAKING UP

Seam the two pieces of the mitre together. Sew an 8-mm (5/16-inch) and the 5-mm (3/16-inch) sequins onto the mitre, securing each with a gold bead.

To finish, thread the cross-shaped charm on a short length of the gold metallic embroidery thread and tie round the Archbishop's neck.

Prince Harry
WILLIAM'S SUPPORTER

The groom's younger brother, known as Prince Harry (though his real name is Henry), will be one of his supporters, the royal equivalent of a best man. Harry is knitted here in the dress uniform of the Blues and Royals of the Household Cavalry Regiment, for whom he is a tank commander and has seen recent active service. He is also an Army Air Corps helicopter pilot.

DOLL

HEAD
The head is knitted from the forehead down to the chin.
Make 2 pieces
- Cast on 12 sts in pale flesh.
- Work 12 rows in st st beg with a K row.
- Next row: K1, m1, K10, m1, K1. [14 sts]
- Work 7 rows in st st beg with a P row.
- Cast (bind) off.

EARS
Make 2
- Cast on 4 sts in pale flesh.
- 1st row: (k2tog) twice. [2 sts]
- Next row: p2tog.
- Break yarn and pull it through rem st.

BODY
The body is knitted from the lower edge to the neck edge.
Make 2 pieces
- Cast on 14 sts in pale flesh.
- Work 20 rows in st st beg with a K row.
- Next row: Cast (bind) off 1 st, K to end. [13 sts]
- Next row: Cast (bind) off 1 st pwise, P to end. [12 sts]
- Cast (bind) off.

You will need

FOR THE DOLL
25 g (1 oz), approx. 40 m/44 yds, of pale flesh DK yarn
A small amount of black DK yarn
A small amount of orange DK yarn
Very small amounts of cream and red DK yarn
10–15 g (¼–½ oz) polyester toy stuffing

FOR THE CLOTHES
20 g (¾ oz), approx. 49 m/54 yds, of dark navy DK yarn
A small amount of red DK yarn
A small amount of black DK yarn
A small amount of dark red embroidery thread
A small amount of gold crochet yarn
Twelve 4-mm (5/32-inch) gold beads for the buttons
A 3-mm (1/8-inch) gold bead for securing the cap badge
Four 5-mm (3/16-inch) gold sequins for the medals and cap badge
An 18-cm (7-inch) length of 9-mm (11/32-inch) wide gold ribbon for the sash
A small piece of striped ribbon for the medals

Use size 3 mm (US 2 or 3) knitting needles

LEGS & SHOES

The legs and shoes are knitted as one piece, from the sole of the shoe to the top of the thigh.

Make 2

- Cast on 28 sts in black.
- Work 4 rows in st st beg with a K row.
- Next row: K6, cast (bind) off 16 sts, K to end. [12 sts]
- Next row: P.
- Break yarn and join pale flesh yarn.
- Work 24 rows in st st beg with a K row.
- Cast (bind) off loosely.

ARMS

The arms are knitted from the top of the shoulder to the tip of the hand.

Make 2

- Cast on 9 sts in pale flesh.
- Work 24 rows in st st beg with a K row.
- Next row: K2, k2tog, K1, ssk, K2. [7 sts]
- Next row: p2tog, P3, p2tog. [5 sts]
- Cast (bind) off loosely.

MAKING UP

Stitch the doll together as described on page 16.

FEATURES

Embroider the nose in chain stitch using pale flesh yarn. Using black yarn, embroider two French knots for the eyes. Using cream yarn, work a ring of chain stitch round each French knot. Separate a short length of red yarn lengthwise so you have two thinner lengths of yarn. Use one length to work two straight stitches for the mouth. Use a red colouring pencil to colour the cheeks.

HAIR

- Cast on 10 sts in orange.
- K 1 row but instead of winding yarn round a single time to work each stitch, wind it round three times.
- Next row: K each st, pulling all three loops off the left-hand needle as you knit. (By the end of the row you will have a series of vertical threads between the 2 rows of your knitting.)
- Cast (bind) off.

Fold the piece in half lengthwise and fasten to the top of the head using the photograph on page 17 as a guide, with the cast-off edge at the front of the head, just below the top seam.

TROUSERS

The trousers are knitted as one piece.

Make 1

- Cast on 14 sts for first leg in navy.
- 1st row: K.
- Next row: P.
- K 2 rows.
- Work 24 rows in st st beg with a K row.
- Break yarn and leave sts on a spare needle or stitch holder.
- Work a second trouser leg exactly as the first but don't break yarn.
- Next row: K 14 sts from second trouser leg then knit across 14 sts from first trouser leg. [28 sts]
- Work 9 rows in st st beg with a P row.
- Next row: (K1, P1) to end.
- Rep last row once more.
- Cast (bind) off quite loosely, keeping to the K1, P1 pattern.

MAKING UP

Seam the trousers together as described on page 17. Using red yarn, embroider a row of chain stitch down the sides of the trouser legs.

JACKET

The two front sides and the back of the jacket are knitted as one piece, from the lower edge to the neck edge.

Make 1

- Cast on 30 sts in dark navy.
- K 2 rows.
- Next and every ws row: K1, P to last st, K1.
- Work 10 rows in st st beg with a K row, remembering to K2 sts at beg and end of every ws row.
- Next rs row: K6, k2tog, K14, k2tog, K6. [28 sts]
- Work 3 rows as set.
- Next rs row: K6, m1, K16, m1, K6. [30 sts]
- Work 5 rows as set.
- Next row: K8, turn and work on these sts only, leaving rem sts on needle.
- Next row: P to last st, K1.
- Next row: K.
- Next row: P to last st, K1.
- Rep last 2 rows once more.
- Next row: K.
- Break yarn and leave sts on needle.
- With rs facing you, join yarn to rem sts.
- Next row: K14, turn and work on these sts only.
- Work 6 rows in st st beg with a P row.
- Break yarn and leave sts on needle.
- With rs facing you, join yarn to rem 8 sts on left-hand needle.
- Next row: K.
- Next row: K1, P to end.
- Next row: K.
- Rep last 2 rows twice more.
- Now work across all 30 sts on needle.
- Next row: Cast (bind) off 2 sts kwise, P7 [8 sts on needle, including rem st from casting (binding) off], (p2tog) twice, P2, (p2tog) twice, P to end. [24 sts]
- Next row: Cast (bind) off 2 sts, k2tog, K to end. [21 sts]

- Next row: P.
- Next row: k2tog, K to last 2 sts, k2tog. [19 sts]
- Cast (bind) off kwise.

POCKETS
Make 4
- Cast on 6 sts in dark navy.
- Work 5 rows in st st beg with a K row.
- Next row: K.
- Cast (bind) off.

SLEEVES
Make 2
- Cast on 12 sts in dark navy.
- K 2 rows.
- Work 23 rows in st st beg with a P row.
- Cast (bind) off loosely.

MAKING UP
Join the jacket pieces together as described on page 17.

DECORATION
Sew five of the 4-mm (5/32-inch) gold beads down the right front edge of Harry's jacket. Sew a 4-mm (5/32-inch) gold bead onto three of the pockets (omitting Harry's left breast pocket where the medals will be). The jacket can be fastened by using small gaps between stitches on the left front edge of the jacket as buttonholes. Sew two 4-mm (5/32-inch) gold beads at each of the cuffs. Sew three gold sequins onto a small piece of striped ribbon, so that they overlap slightly, to represent the medals. Sew or stick the ribbon and sequins in place on the left breast pocket.

For each epaulette, work three long straight stitches, one over the other, using gold crochet yarn.

For the sash, using three strands of red embroidery thread, work a line of running stitch along the middle of the gold ribbon. Thread the ribbon through Harry's left epaulette, then under his right arm. Glue or stitch the ribbon at the back. You may need to make a small pleat under the arm to ensure that the sash sits flat against the body.

CAP
The cap is knitted in two main parts: the side band and the tip. The peak is knitted onto the side band once the two main parts of the cap have been stitched together.

SIDE BAND
- Cast on 22 sts in black.
- 1st row: K.
- Break yarn and join red yarn.
- Next row: P.
- Next row: K1, (m1, K1) to end. [43 sts]
- Next row: P.
- Break yarn and join dark navy yarn.
- Work 2 rows in st st beg with a K row.
- Cast (bind) off kwise.

TIP
- Cast on 12 sts in dark navy.
- 1st row: K1, inc1, K to last 2 sts, inc1, K1. [14 sts]
- Next row: P.
- Next row: K1, m1, K to last st, m1, K1. [16 sts]
- Next row: P.
- Rep last 2 rows twice more. [20 sts]
- Work 4 rows in st st beg with a K row.
- Next row: K1, k2tog, K to last 3 sts, ssk, K1. [18 sts]
- Next row: P.
- Rep last 2 rows twice more. [14 sts]
- Next row: K1, k2tog, K to last 3 sts, ssk, K1. [12 sts]
- Cast (bind) off kwise.

Join the short sides of the side band to form a circle and oversew the tip in place from the inside, so the rows of knitting lie across the width of the cap.

PEAK
- Using black yarn and with the rs of the cap facing you, pick up and knit 13 sts across the lower edge of the front of the side band, from one side to the other.
- Next row: P.
- Next row: K1, k2tog, K to last 3 sts, ssk, K1. [11 sts]
- Next row: P.
- Rep last 2 rows once more. [9 sts]
- Next row: K1, m1, K to last st, m1, K1. [11 sts]
- Next row: P.
- Rep last 2 rows once more. [13 sts]
- Cast (bind) off.

Fold the cast-off edge of the peak under. Oversew the sides of the peak together and oversew the cast-off edge of the peak to the inside of the side band.

Using gold crochet yarn, work a line of chain stitch round the outer edge of the peak. Separate a length of red DK yarn lengthwise into two thinner lengths. Use this to embroider a ring of chain stitches round the top of the cap. Sew a sequin at the front of the hat band to represent the badge, securing it with the 3-mm (1/8-inch) gold bead.

Elizabeth II
THE QUEEN

Queen Elizabeth II is the groom's grandmother. She has been the Queen of England and official head of state since 1952 and is one of the UK's longest ever reigning monarchs. Shown here dressed for the occasion in one of her favourite colours and styles of hat, she is equally at home in a riding outfit or in country tweeds, out for a walk with her beloved corgis.

DOLL
HEAD
The head is knitted from the chin up to the forehead.
Make 2 pieces
- Cast on 8 sts in beige.
- 1st row: K1, inc1, K to last st, inc1, K1. [10 sts]
- Next row: P.
- Next row: K1, m1, K to last st, m1, K1. [12 sts]
- Next row: P.
- Rep last 2 rows once more. [14 sts]
- Work 4 rows in st st beg with a K row.
- Next row: K2, k2tog, K6, ssk, K2. [12 sts]
- Work 5 rows in st st beg with a P row.
- Next row: K1, k2tog, K6, ssk, K1. [10 sts]
- Next row: p2tog, P6, p2tog. [8 sts]
- Cast (bind) off.

BODY
The body is knitted from the lower edge to the neck edge.
Make 2 pieces
- Cast on 14 sts in beige.
- Work 6 rows in st st beg with a K row.

- Next row: K2, k2tog, K6, ssk, K2. [12 sts]
- Next row: P.
- Next row: K2, k2tog, K4, ssk, K2. [10 sts]
- Next row: P.
- Next row: K2, m1, K6, m1, K2. [12 sts]
- Work 5 rows in st st beg with a P row.
- Next row: Cast (bind) off 1 st, K to end. [11 sts]
- Next row: Cast (bind) off 1 st pwise, P to end. [10 sts]
- Cast (bind) off.

LEGS
The legs are knitted as one piece, from the sole of the foot to the top of the thigh.
Make 2
- Cast on 20 sts in beige.
- Work 4 rows in st st beg with a K row.
- Next row: K5, cast (bind) off 10 sts, K to end. [10 sts]
- Work 19 rows in st st beg with a P row.
- Cast (bind) off loosely.

ARMS
The arms are knitted from the top of the shoulder to the tip of the hand.
Make 2
- Cast on 9 sts in beige.
- Work 24 rows in st st beg with a K row.
- Next row: K2, k2tog, K1, ssk, K2. [7 sts]
- Next row: p2tog, P3, p2tog. [5 sts]
- Cast (bind) off loosely.

MAKING UP
Stitch the doll together as described on page 16.

FEATURES
Embroider the nose in chain stitch using beige yarn. Using black yarn, embroider two French knots for the eyes. Using cream yarn, work a ring of chain stitch round each French knot. Separate a short length of red yarn lengthwise so you have two thinner

lengths of yarn. Use one length to work two straight stitches for the mouth. Use a red colouring pencil to colour the cheeks.

HAIR
The hair is knitted as one piece beginning at the fringe (bangs).
- Cast on 8 sts in pale grey.
- Work 12 rows in st st beg with a K row.
- Next row: Cast on 10 sts, K to end. [18 sts]
- Next row: Cast on 10 sts, P to end. [28 sts]
- Work 4 rows in st st beg with a K row.
- Next row: Cast (bind) off 10 sts, K to end. [18 sts]
- Next row: Cast (bind) off 10 sts pwise, P to end. [8 sts]
- Work 10 rows in st st beg with a K row.
- Cast (bind) off.

To make up, seam the piece into a box shape but leave the top 1 cm (3/8 inch) of the front part of the 'box' free. Roll under the fringe (bangs) and secure. Roll up the sides and back of the hair. To keep her hair in shape, spray with water and dry before stitching in place.

DRESS
The front and back of the dress are identical.
Make 2 pieces
- Cast on 16 sts in royal blue.
- 1st row: P.
- K 3 rows.
- Work 11 rows in st st beg with a P row.
- Next row: K2, ssk, K8, k2tog, K2. [14 sts]
- Next row: P.
- Next row: K2, ssk, K6, k2tog, K2. [12 sts]
- Work 5 rows in st st beg with a K row.
- Next row: K2, m1, K8, m1, K2. [14 sts]
- Next row: P.
- Next row: K2, m1, K10, m1, K2. [16 sts]
- Work 3 rows in st st beg with a P row.
- Next row: k2tog, K3, cast (bind) off 6 sts, K to last 2 sts, ssk.

- Turn and cont on last 4 sts only, leaving other sts on the needle.
- Next row: p2tog, P2. [3 sts]
- Next row: K.
- Next row: P.
- Next row: k2tog, K1. [2 sts]
- Next row: P.
- Next row: k2tog, break yarn and pull tail through rem st.
- With ws facing you, join yarn to rem 4 sts.
- Next row: P2, p2tog. [3 sts]
- Next row: K.
- Next row: P.
- Next row: K1, k2tog. [2 sts]
- Next row: P.
- Next row: k2tog, break yarn and pull tail through rem st.

MAKING UP
Seam the dress together as described on page 17.

COAT
The two front sides and the back of the coat are knitted as one piece, from the lower edge to the neck edge.
Make 1
- Cast on 40 sts in royal blue.
- 1st row: K2, P to last 2 sts, K2.
- K 3 rows.
- Next row: K2, P to last 2 sts, K2.
- Next row: K.
- Next row: K2, P to last 2 sts, K2.
- Rep last 2 rows once more.
- Next row: K9, ssk, K18, k2tog, K9. [38 sts]
- Next and every ws row: K2, P to last 2 sts, K2.
- Work 2 rows as set.
- Next rs row: K8, (ssk) twice, K14, (k2tog) twice, K8. [34 sts]
- Work 3 rows as set.
- Next rs row: K7, (ssk) twice, K12, (k2tog) twice, K7. [30 sts]

- Work 3 rows as set.
- Next rs row: K6, (ssk) twice, K10, (k2tog) twice, K6. [26 sts]
- Work 5 rows as set.
- Next rs row: K7, turn and work on these sts only, leaving rem sts on needle.
- Next row: P to last 2 sts, K2.
- Next row: K.
- Rep last 2 rows once more.
- Next row: P to last 2 sts, K2.
- Next row: Cast (bind) off 2 sts, K to end. [5 sts]
- Break yarn and leave rem 5 sts on stitch holder or large safety pin.
- With rs facing you, join yarn to rem 19 sts on needle.
- Next row: K12, turn and work on these sts only, leaving rem sts on needle.
- Work 6 rows in st st beg with a P row.
- Break yarn and leave rem sts on needle.
- With rs facing you, join yarn to rem 7 sts on needle.
- Next row: K.
- Next row: K2, P to end.
- Rep last 2 rows twice more.
- Next row: K.
- Next row: Cast (bind) off 2 sts kwise, P4 [5 sts on needle, including rem st from casting (binding) off], then P 12 sts on needle and then 5 sts on holder. [22 sts]
- K 4 rows.
- Cast (bind) off.

SLEEVES
Make 2
- Cast on 12 sts in royal blue.
- K 4 rows.
- Work 11 rows in st st beg with a P row.
- Cast (bind) off loosely.

MAKING UP
Seam the coat together as described on page 17 and sew on the buttons.

HAT
- Cast on 30 sts in royal blue.
- Work 4 rows in st st beg with a K row.
- Next row: Cast (bind) off 12 sts, K to last 12 sts, cast (bind) off last 12 sts.
- Break yarn and with ws facing you, join yarn to rem 6 sts.
- Next row: P.
- Next row: K1, m1, K to last 2 sts, m1, K1. [8 sts]
- Next row: P.
- Rep last 2 rows once more. [10 sts]
- Work 2 rows in st st beg with a K row.
- Next row: K1, ssk, K to last 3 sts, k2tog, K1. [8 sts]
- Next row: P.
- Next row: K1, ssk, K to last 3 sts, k2tog, K1. [6 sts]
- Cast (bind) off pwise.
- With rs of top part of hat facing you, pick up and K 30 sts along cast-on edge.
- Next row: P.
- Next row: K1, (inc1, K1) 28 times, K1. [58 sts]
- Work 4 rows in st st beg with a P row.
- Cast (bind) off loosely pwise.

MAKING UP
Join the back seam of the hat and oversew the top part of the hat to the side band. Tie the blue ribbon round the hat, making a bow at the front, and secure in place.

SHOES
The shoes are knitted from the top edge to the bottom edge.
Make 2
- Using size 2.25 mm (US 1) needles, cast on 24 sts in black silk rayon embroidery thread.
- Work 5 rows in st st beg with a K row.
- Next row: K.
- Cast (bind) off.

MAKING UP
Fold the strip widthways so that the right sides are together. Oversew the short edge and bottom seam (cast-off edge). Oversew just under 1 cm (³/₈ inch) of the top seam (cast-on) edge to form the toe section. Turn the shoe the right way out.

BAG
The bag is knitted as one piece, from the top of the opening of the bag to the tip of the flap.
- Cast on 9 sts in black.
- Work 4 rows in st st beg with a K row.
- Next row: K1, m1, K7, m1, K1. [11 sts]
- Work 5 rows in st st beg with a P row.
- Next row: K1, ssk, K5, k2tog, K1. [9 sts]
- Work 5 rows in st st beg with a P row.
- Next row: K1, ssk, K3, k2tog, K1. [7 sts]
- Next row: P.
- Next row: K1, ssk, K1, k2tog, K1. [5 sts]
- Cast (bind) off kwise.

For the handles, crochet a 5.5-cm (2¼-inch) chain in gold embroidery thread.

MAKING UP
Fold the cast-on edge upwards so that it is level with what will be the top of the bag and the right sides of the bag are together. Oversew the side seams and turn the right way out. Fasten the ends of the handle to the sides of the bag, securing the 'tails' in the inside seams. Sew the gold bead on the top flap of the bag.

To finish, double the bracelet and put it round the doll's neck. Sew on the pearls for earrings. Fasten the diamond jewel on the doll's right-hand lapel.

Prince Philip
DUKE OF EDINBURGH

Nearly 90 years old, Prince Philip, the Duke of Edinburgh, is as feisty as ever. Born in Corfu, Prince Philip is the great-great-grandson of Queen Victoria. With an active naval career behind him, he is an Admiral of the Fleet and is shown here in a knitted version of his full naval uniform and the blue sash of the Order of the Garter.

DOLL

HEAD
The head is knitted from the chin up to the forehead.
Make 2 pieces
- Cast on 10 sts in beige.
- Work 2 rows in st st beg with a K row.
- Next row: K1, m1, K8, m1, K1. [12 sts]
- Work 17 rows in st st beg with a P row.
- Cast (bind) off.

EARS
Make 2
- Cast on 4 sts in beige.
- 1st row: (k2tog) twice. [2 sts]
- Next row: p2tog.
- Break yarn and pull it through rem st.

BODY
The body is knitted from the lower edge to the neck edge.
Make 2 pieces
- Cast on 14 sts in beige.
- Work 20 rows in st st beg with a K row.
- Next row: Cast (bind) off 1 st, K to end. [13 sts]
- Next row: Cast (bind) off 1 st pwise, P to end. [12 sts]
- Cast (bind) off.

You will need

FOR THE DOLL
25 g (1 oz), approx. 40 m/44 yds, of beige DK yarn
A small amount of black DK yarn
A small amount of pale grey DK yarn
Very small amounts of cream and red DK yarn
10–15 g (¼–½ oz) polyester toy stuffing

❧

FOR THE CLOTHES
20 g (¾ oz), approx. 46 m/50 yds, of navy DK yarn
A small amount of ochre DK yarn
A small amount of white DK yarn
A small amount of gold crochet yarn
A length of gold embroidery thread
Thirteen 3-mm (⅛-inch) gold beads for the buttons and securing some of the sequins
Two 10-mm (⅜-inch) star-shaped silver sequins for the medals
A 22-cm (8¾-inch) length of 12-mm (½-inch) wide royal blue ribbon for the sash
Nine 5-mm (³⁄₁₆-inch) gold sequins for the belt buckle and medals
A small piece of striped ribbon for the medals
A 15-cm (6-inch) length of ready-made gold bead trimming for the neck chain
An 8-mm (⁵⁄₁₆-inch) gold sequin for the cap badge

❧

Use size 3 mm (US 2 or 3) knitting needles and a size 3.25 mm (US D-3) crochet hook

LEGS & SHOES

The legs and shoes are knitted as one piece, from the shoe to the top of the thigh.
Make 2

- Cast on 28 sts in black.
- Work 4 rows in st st beg with a K row.
- Next row: K6, cast (bind) off 16 sts, K to end. [12 sts]
- Next row: P.
- Break yarn and join beige yarn.
- Work 24 rows in st st beg with a K row.
- Cast (bind) off loosely.

ARMS

The arms are knitted from the top of the shoulder to the tip of the hand.
Make 2

- Cast on 9 sts in beige.
- Work 24 rows in st st beg with a K row.
- Next row: K2, k2tog, K1, ssk, K2. [7 sts]
- Next row: p2tog, P3, p2tog. [5 sts]
- Cast (bind) off loosely.

MAKING UP

Stitch the doll together as described on page 16.

FEATURES

Embroider the nose in chain stitch using beige yarn. Using black yarn, embroider two French knots for the eyes. Using cream yarn, work a ring of chain stitch round each French knot. Using pale grey yarn, work a single straight stitch across the top part of each eye for the eyebrows. Separate a short length of red yarn lengthwise so you have two thinner lengths of yarn. Use one length to work two straight stitches for the mouth. Use a red colouring pencil to colour the cheeks.

HAIR

Using pale grey yarn, work a few straight stitches round the sides and back of the head for the hair.

TROUSERS

The trousers are knitted as one piece.
Make 1

- Cast on 14 sts for first leg in navy.
- 1st row: K.
- Next row: P.
- K 2 rows.
- Work 24 rows in st st beg with a K row.
- Break yarn and leave sts on spare needle or stitch holder.
- Work a second trouser leg exactly as the first but don't break yarn.
- Next row: K 14 sts from second trouser leg then knit across 14 sts from first trouser leg. [28 sts]
- Work 9 rows in st st beg with a P row.
- Next row: (K1, P1) to end.
- Rep last row once more.
- Cast (bind) off quite loosely, keeping to the K1, P1 pattern.

MAKING UP

Seam the trousers together as described on page 17. Using ochre yarn, embroider a row of chain stitch down the sides of the trousers.

JACKET

The two front sides and the back of the jacket are knitted as one piece, from the lower edge to the neck edge.
Make 1

- Cast on 8 sts in navy.
- 1st row: K1, inc1, K to last 2 sts, inc1, K to end. [10 sts]
- Next row: K1, P to last st, K1.
- Next row: K1, m1, K to last st, m1, K1. [12 sts]
- Next row: K1, P to last st, K1.
- Rep last 2 rows three times more. [18 sts]
- Next row: K.
- Next row: K1, P to last st, K1.
- Rep last 2 rows four times more.

- Next row: Cast on 9 sts, K to end. [27 sts]
- Next row: Cast on 9 sts, K1, P to last st, K1. [36 sts]
- Next row: K.
- Next row: K1, P to last st, K1.
- Rep last 2 rows three times more.
- Next row: K11, turn and work on these sts only, leaving rem sts on needle.
- Next row: P to last st, K1.
- Next row: K.
- Next row: P to last st, K1.
- Rep last 2 rows once more.
- Next row: K.
- Break yarn and leave sts on needle.
- With rs facing you, join yarn to rem sts.
- Next row: K14, turn and work on these sts only.
- Work 6 rows in st st beg with a P row.
- Break yarn and leave sts on needle.
- With rs facing you, join yarn to rem 11 sts on left-hand needle
- Next row: K.
- Next row: K1, P to end.
- Next row: K.
- Rep last 2 rows twice more.
- Now work across all 36 sts on needle.
- Next row: Cast (bind) off 5 sts kwise, P7 [8 sts on needle, including rem st from casting (binding) off], (p2tog) twice, P2, (p2tog) twice, P to end. [27 sts]
- Next row: Cast (bind) off 5 sts, break yarn and join white yarn, K1, then pass the rem navy st over the st just knitted, K to end. [21 sts]
- Next row: P.
- Next row: k2tog, K to last 2 sts, k2tog. [19 sts]
- Cast (bind) off kwise.

SLEEVES
Make 2
- Cast on 12 sts in navy.
- K 2 rows.
- Work 23 rows in st st beg with a P row.
- Cast (bind) off loosely.

BELT
Make 1
- Cast on 32 sts in black.
- Cast (bind) off.

MAKING UP
Before joining the jacket pieces, separate a length of ochre yarn lengthwise so you have two thinner lengths of yarn. Use these to work five rows of chain stitch at the cuff edge of each sleeve. In the row furthest from the cuff, make a small loop of stitching as shown in the photograph on page 39. Now join the jacket pieces together as described on page 17.

DECORATION
Sew a row of five gold beads down the front edge of the left-hand side of Philip's jacket. Sew another row of five beads to match, approximately 2.5 cm (1 inch) over on the same side. Sew the two star-shaped silver sequins on the left-hand side of the jacket, securing each with a gold bead. For each epaulette, work three long straight stitches, one over the other, using gold crochet yarn.

For the sash, thread the blue ribbon through Philip's left epaulette and tie at the opposite side.

Sew eight gold sequins onto a small piece of striped ribbon, so that they overlap slightly, to represent the prince's numerous medals and honours. Sew or stick the ribbon and sequins in place. Thread the gold bead trimming through the epaulettes and fasten it round Philip's neck. For the

chain on Philip's right shoulder, make a 13-cm (5-inch) crochet chain using gold crochet yarn. Thread the middle of the chain just under the right epaulette and secure. Secure the ends of the chain to the jacket front close to the top two buttons, using the photograph as a guide, and trim the ends to approximately 2 cm (¾ inch).

Using gold embroidery thread, run a line of running stitches round the length of the belt.

Join the two short ends together and sew a gold sequin in the centre front of the belt for the buckle.

CAP
The cap is knitted in two main parts – the side band and the tip. The peak is knitted onto the side band once the two main parts of the cap have been stitched together.

SIDE BAND
- Cast on 22 sts in navy.
- K 2 rows.
- Next row: P.
- Break yarn and join white yarn.
- Work 2 rows in st st beg with a K row.
- Next row: K1, (m1, K1) to end. [43 sts]
- Next row: P.
- Cast (bind) off kwise.

TIP
- Cast on 12 sts in white.
- 1st row: K1, inc1, K to last 2 sts, inc1, K1. [14 sts]
- Next row: P.
- Next row: K1, m1, K to last st, m1, K1. [16 sts]
- Next row: P.
- Rep last 2 rows twice more. [20 sts]
- Work 4 rows in st st beg with a K row.
- Next row: K1, k2tog, K to last 3 sts, ssk, K1. [18 sts]

- Next row: P.
- Rep last 2 rows twice more. [14 sts]
- Next row: K1, k2tog, K to last 3 sts, ssk, K1. [12 sts]
- Cast (bind) off kwise.

Join the short sides of the side band to form a circle and oversew the tip in place from the inside, so the rows of knitting lie across the width of the cap.

PEAK
- Using navy yarn and with the rs of the cap facing you, pick up and knit 13 sts across the lower edge of the front of the side band, from one side to the other.
- Next row: P.
- Next row: K1, k2tog, K to last 3 sts, ssk, K1. [11 sts]
- Next row: P.
- Rep last 2 rows once more. [9 sts]
- Next row: K1, m1, K to last st, m1, K1. [11 sts]
- Next row: P.
- Next row: K1, m1, K to last st, m1, K1. [13 sts]
- Cast (bind) off.

Fold the cast-off edge of the peak under. Oversew the sides of the peak together and the cast-off edge of the peak to the inside of the side band.

Using gold crochet yarn, work a line of chain stitches round the entire peak. Using navy yarn, work a small circle of chain stitches on the front of the cap, just big enough to surround the gold sequin. Sew the sequin in the centre of the circle, securing it with a gold bead.

Charles

PRINCE OF WALES

Prince Charles, the groom's father, is first in line to the throne. He is well known for his charity work, particularly in the environment and youth enterprise sectors. Like his own father, he had a naval career, so he's dressed here in a knitted version of his full naval uniform and the blue sash of the Order of the Garter.

You will need

FOR THE DOLL

25 g (1 oz), approx. 40 m/44 yds,
of beige DK yarn

A small amount of black DK yarn

A small amount of dark grey DK yarn

Very small amounts of cream and red DK yarn

10–15 g (¼–½ oz) polyester toy stuffing

FOR THE CLOTHES

20 g (¾ oz), approx. 46 m/50 yds,
of navy DK yarn

A small amount of ochre DK yarn

A small amount of white DK yarn

A small amount of gold crochet yarn

Thirteen 3-mm (⅛-inch) gold beads for the buttons and securing some of the sequins

Two 10-mm (⅜-inch) star-shaped
silver sequins for the jacket medals

A 22-cm (8¾-inch) length of 12-mm (½-inch)
wide royal blue ribbon for the sash

Six 5-mm (³⁄₁₆-inch) gold sequins
for the belt buckle and medals

A small piece of striped ribbon
for the medals

A small star-shaped yellow button for a medal

An 8-mm (⁵⁄₁₆-inch) gold sequin for the hat badge

Use size 3 mm (US 2 or 3) knitting needles
and a size 3.25 mm (US D-3) crochet hook

DOLL

HEAD
The head is knitted from the chin
up to the forehead.
Make 2 pieces
- Cast on 10 sts in beige.
- Work 2 rows in st st beg with a K row.
- Next row: K1, m1, K8, m1, K1.
  [12 sts]
- Work 17 rows in st st beg with a
  P row.
- Cast (bind) off.

EARS
Make 2
- Cast on 4 sts in beige.
- 1st row: (k2tog) twice. [2 sts]
- Next row: p2tog.
- Break yarn and pull it through
  rem st.

BODY
The body is worked from the
lower edge to the shoulder edge.
Make 2 pieces
- Cast on 14 sts in beige.
- Work 18 rows in st st beg with a K row.
- Next row: Cast (bind) off 1 st, K to end.
  [13 sts]
- Next row: Cast (bind) off 1 st pwise,
  P to end. [12 sts]
- Cast (bind) off.

LEGS & SHOES

The legs and shoes are knitted as one piece, from the sole of the shoe to the top of the thigh.

Make 2

- Cast on 28 sts in black.
- Work 4 rows in st st beg with a K row.
- Next row: K6, cast (bind) off 16 sts, K to end. [12 sts]
- Next row: P.
- Break yarn and join beige yarn.
- Work 24 rows in st st beg with a K row.
- Cast (bind) off loosely.

ARMS

The arms are knitted from the top of the shoulder to the tip of the hand.

Make 2

- Cast on 9 sts in beige.
- Work 24 rows in st st beg with a K row.
- Next row: K2, k2tog, K1, ssk, K2. [7 sts]
- Next row: p2tog, P3, p2tog. [5 sts]
- Cast (bind) off loosely.

MAKING UP

Stitch the doll together as described on page 16.

FEATURES

Embroider the nose in chain stitch using beige yarn. Using black yarn, embroider two French knots for the eyes. Using cream yarn, work a ring of chain stitch round each French knot. Separate a short length of red yarn lengthwise so you have two thinner lengths of yarn. Use one length to work two straight stitches for the mouth. Use a red colouring pencil to colour the cheeks.

HAIR

Using dark grey yarn, embroider a few lines of chain stitch on top of Charles's head for his hair.

TROUSERS

The trousers are knitted as one piece.

Make 1

- Cast on 14 sts for first leg in navy.
- 1st row: K.
- Next row: P.
- K 2 rows.
- Work 24 rows in st st beg with a K row.
- Break yarn and leave sts on spare needle or stitch holder.
- Work a second trouser leg exactly as the first but don't break yarn.
- Next row: K 14 sts from second trouser leg then knit across 14 sts from first trouser leg. [28 sts]
- Work 9 rows in st st beg with a P row.
- Next row: (K1, P1) to end.
- Rep last row once more.
- Cast (bind) off quite loosely, keeping to the K1, P1 pattern.

MAKING UP

Seam the trousers together as described on page 17. Using ochre yarn, embroider a row of chain stitch down the sides of the trouser legs.

JACKET

The two front sides and the back of the jacket are knitted as one piece, from the lower edge to the neck edge.

Make 1

- Cast on 8 sts in navy.
- 1st row: K1, inc1, K to last 2 sts, inc1, K to end. [10 sts]
- Next row: K1, P to last st, K1.
- Next row: K1, m1, K to last st, m1, K1. [12 sts]
- Next row: K1, P to last st, K1.
- Rep last 2 rows three times more. [18 sts]
- Next row: K.
- Next row: K1, P to last st, K1.
- Rep last 2 rows four times more.

- Next row: Cast on 9 sts, K to end. [27 sts]
- Next row: Cast on 9 sts, K1, P to last st, K1. [36 sts]
- Next row: K.
- Next row: K1, P to last st, K1.
- Rep last 2 rows three times more.
- Next row: K11, turn and work on these sts only, leaving rem sts on needle.
- Next row: P to last st, K1.
- Next row: K.
- Next row: P to last st, K1.
- Rep last 2 rows once more.
- Next row: K.
- Break yarn and leave sts on needle.
- With rs facing you, join yarn to rem sts.
- Next row: K14, turn and work on these sts only.
- Work 6 rows in st st beg with a P row.
- Break yarn and leave sts on needle.
- With rs facing you, join yarn to rem 11 sts on left-hand needle.
- Next row: K.
- Next row: K1, P to end.
- Next row: K.
- Rep last 2 rows twice more.
- Now work across all 36 sts on needle.
- Next row: Cast (bind) off 5 sts kwise, P7 [8 sts on needle, including rem st from casting (binding) off], (p2tog) twice, P2, (p2tog) twice, P to end. [27 sts]
- Next row: Cast (bind) off 5 sts, break yarn and join white yarn, K1, then pass the rem navy st over the st just knitted, K to end. [21 sts]
- Next row: P.
- Next row: k2tog, K to last 2 sts, k2tog. [19 sts]
- Cast (bind) off kwise.

SLEEVES

Make 2

- Cast on 12 sts in navy.
- K 2 rows.
- Work 23 rows in st st beg with a P row.
- Cast (bind) off loosely.

BELT

Make 2

- Cast on 32 sts in gold crochet yarn.
- Cast (bind) off.

MAKING UP

Before joining the jacket pieces, separate a length of ochre yarn lengthwise so you have two thinner lengths of yarn. Use these to work four rows of chain stitch at the cuff edge of each sleeve. In the row furthest from the cuff, make a small loop of stitching as shown in the photograph on page 42. Now join the jacket pieces together as described on page 17.

DECORATION

Sew a row of five gold beads down the front edge of the left-hand side of Charles's jacket. Sew another row of five beads to match, approximately 2.5 cm (1 inch) over on the same side. Sew the two star-shaped silver sequins on the left-hand side of the jacket, securing each with a gold bead. For each epaulette, work three long straight stitches, one over the other, using gold crochet yarn.

For the sash, thread the blue ribbon through Charles's left epaulette and tie at the opposite side.

Sew five gold sequins onto a small piece of striped ribbon, so that they overlap slightly, to represent the medals. Sew or stick the ribbon and sequins in place. For the chain on Charles's right shoulder, make a 13-cm (5-inch) crochet chain using gold crochet yarn. Thread the

middle of the chain just under the right epaulette and secure. Secure the ends of the chain to the jacket front and trim the ends to approximately 2 cm (¾ inch). Sew the star-shaped button to the front of the jacket.

Join the two short ends of the belt together and sew a gold sequin in the centre front of the belt for the buckle.

CAP

The cap is knitted in two main parts – the side band and the tip. The peak is knitted onto the side band once the two main parts of the cap have been stitched together.

SIDE BAND

- Cast on 22 sts in navy.
- K 2 rows.
- Next row: P.
- Break yarn and join white yarn.
- Work 2 rows in st st beg with a K row.
- Next row: K1, (m1, K1) to end. [43 sts]
- Next row: P.
- Cast (bind) off kwise.

TIP

- Cast on 12 sts in white.
- 1st row: K1, inc1, K to last 2 sts, inc1, K1. [14 sts]
- Next row: P.
- Next row: K1, m1, K to last st, m1, K1. [16 sts]
- Next row: P.
- Rep last 2 rows twice more. [20 sts]
- Work 4 rows in st st beg with a K row.
- Next row: K1, k2tog, K to last 3 sts, ssk, K1. [18 sts]
- Next row: P.
- Rep last 2 rows twice more. [14 sts]
- Next row: K1, k2tog, K to last 3 sts, ssk, K1. [12 sts]
- Cast (bind) off kwise.

Join the short sides of the side band to form a circle and oversew the tip in place from the inside, so the rows of knitting lie across the width of the cap.

PEAK

- Using navy yarn and with the rs of the cap facing you, pick up and knit 13 sts across the lower edge of the front of the side band, from one side to the other.
- Next row: P.
- Next row: K1, k2tog, K to last 3 sts, ssk, K1. [11 sts]
- Next row: P.
- Rep last 2 rows once more. [9 sts]
- Next row: K1, m1, K to last st, m1, K1. [11 sts]
- Next row: P.
- Next row: K1, m1, K to last st, m1, K1. [13 sts]
- Cast (bind) off.

Fold the cast-off edge of the peak under. Oversew the sides of the peak together and the cast-off edge of the peak to the inside of the side band.

Using gold crochet yarn, work a line of chain stitches round the entire peak. Using navy yarn, work a small circle of chain stitches on the front of the hat, just big enough to surround the 8-mm (5/16-inch) gold sequin. Sew the sequin in the centre of the circle, securing it with a 3-mm (1/8-inch) gold bead.

Camilla
DUCHESS OF CORNWALL

The Duchess of Cornwall, Prince Charles's second wife and the groom's stepmother, loves horses and riding. She also has two Jack Russell terriers and shares her husband's love of the arts and gardening. She has a penchant for fancy hats and is shown here in a knitted version, complete with jaunty feather, to match her clothes.

DOLL

HEAD

The head is knitted from the base of the chin to the top of the forehead.

Make 2 pieces

- Cast on 6 sts in beige.
- 1st row: K1, inc1, K to last st, inc1, K1. [8 sts]
- Next row: P.
- Next row: K1, m1, K to last st, m1, K1. [10 sts]
- Next row: P.
- Rep last 2 rows twice more. [14 sts]
- Work 10 rows in st st beg with a K row.
- Next row: K2, k2tog, K6, ssk, K2. [12 sts]
- Next row: p2tog, P to last 2 sts, p2tog. [10 sts]
- Cast (bind) off.

BODY

The body is knitted from the lower edge to the neck edge.

Make 2 pieces

- Cast on 14 sts in beige.
- Work 8 rows in st st beg with a K row.
- Next row: K2, (k2tog) twice, K2, (ssk) twice, K2. [10 sts]
- Work 3 rows in st st beg with a P row.

- Next row: K2, m1, K to last 2 sts, m1, K2. [12 sts]
- Next row: P.
- Rep last 2 rows twice more. [16 sts]
- Work 2 rows in st st beg with a K row.
- Next row: Cast (bind) off 1 st, K to end. [13 sts]
- Next row: Cast (bind) off 1 st pwise, P to end. [12 sts]
- Cast (bind) off.

LEGS

The legs are knitted as one piece, from the sole of the foot to the top of the thigh.
Make 2

- Cast on 20 sts in beige.
- Work 4 rows in st st beg with a K row.
- Next row: K5, cast (bind) off 10 sts, K to end. [12 sts]
- Work 19 rows in st st beg with a P row.
- Cast (bind) off loosely.

ARMS

The arms are knitted from the top of the shoulder to the tip of the hand.
Make 2

- Cast on 9 sts in beige.
- Work 24 rows in st st beg with a K row.
- Next row: K2, k2tog, K1, ssk, K2. [7 sts]
- Next row: p2tog, P3, p2tog. [5 sts]
- Cast (bind) off loosely.

MAKING UP

Stitch the doll together as described on page 16.

FEATURES

Embroider the nose in chain stitch using beige yarn. Using black yarn, embroider two French knots for the eyes. Using cream yarn, work a ring of chain stitch round each French knot. Separate a short length of black yarn lengthwise so you have two thinner lengths of yarn. Use the lengths to work a few

straight stitches round each eye for the eyelashes. Use a separated length of red yarn to work two straight stitches for the mouth. Use a red colouring pencil to colour the cheeks.

HAIR

The hair is knitted as one piece beginning at the fringe (bangs).

- Cast on 4 sts in pale yellow.
- Work 10 rows in st st beg with a K row.
- Break yarn and leave sts on needle.
- Work another section as above but do not break yarn.
- Next row: K across all 8 sts.
- Next row: P.
- Next row: Cast on 12 sts, K to end. [20 sts]
- Next row: Cast on 12 sts, P to end. [32 sts]
- Work 4 rows in st st beg with a K row.
- Next row: Cast (bind) off 11 sts, K to end. [21 sts]
- Next row: Cast (bind) off 11 sts pwise, P to end. [10 sts]
- Work 12 rows in st st beg with a K row.
- Cast (bind) off.

MAKING UP

Seam the piece into a box shape but leave the top 1.5 cm (⅝ inch) of the front part of the 'box' (which will form the sides at the front of the hair) free. Roll up the fringe (bangs), the sides and the back of the hair. To keep the hair in shape, spray with water and dry before stitching in place.

DRESS

The front and back of the dress are identical.
Make 2 pieces

- Cast on 16 sts in coral.
- Work 15 rows in st st beg with a P row.
- Next row: K2, ssk, K8, k2tog, K2. [14 sts]
- Next row: P.
- Next row: K2, ssk, K6, k2tog, K2. [12 sts]
- Work 5 rows in st st beg with a K row.

- Next row: K2, m1, K8, m1, K2. [14 sts]
- Next row: P.
- Next row: K2, m1, K10, m1, K2. [16 sts]
- Work 3 rows in st st beg with a P row.
- Next row: k2tog, K3, cast (bind) off 6 sts, K to last 2 sts, ssk.
- Turn and cont on last 4 sts only, leaving other sts on the needle.
- Next row: p2tog, P2. [3 sts]
- Next row: K.
- Next row: P.
- Next row: k2tog, K1. [2 sts]
- Next row: P.
- Next row: k2tog, break yarn and pull tail through rem st.
- With ws facing you, join yarn to rem sts.
- Next row: P2, p2tog. [3 sts]
- Next row: K.
- Next row: P.
- Next row: K1, k2tog. [2 sts]
- Next row: P.
- Next row: k2tog, break yarn and pull tail through rem st.

MAKING UP

Seam the dress together as described on page 17.

COAT

The two front sides and the back of the coat are knitted as one piece, from the lower edge to the neck edge.
Make 1

- Cast on 40 sts in coral.
- 1st row: K2, P to last 2 sts, K2.
- Next row: K.
- Next row: K2, P to last 2 sts, K2.
- Rep last 2 rows four times more.
- Next row: K9, ssk, K18, k2tog, K9. [38 sts]
- Next and every ws row: K2, P to last 2 sts, K2.
- Work 2 rows as set.

- Next rs row: K8, (ssk) twice, K14, (k2tog) twice, K8. [34 sts]
- Work 3 rows as set.
- Next rs row: K7, (ssk) twice, K12, (k2tog) twice, K7. [30 sts]
- Work 3 rows as set.
- Next rs row: K6, (ssk) twice, K10, (k2tog) twice, K6. [26 sts]
- Work 5 rows as set.
- Next rs row: K7, turn and work on these sts only, leaving rem sts on needle.
- Next row: P to last 2 sts, K2.
- Next row: K.
- Rep last 2 rows once more.
- Next row: P to last 2 sts, K2.
- Next row: Cast (bind) off 2 sts, K to end. [5 sts]
- Break yarn and leave rem 5 sts on stitch holder or large safety pin.
- With rs facing you, join yarn to rem 19 sts on needle.
- Next row: K12, turn and work on these sts only, leaving rem sts on needle.
- Work 6 rows in st st beg with a P row.
- Break yarn and leave rem sts on needle.
- With rs facing you, join yarn to rem 7 sts on needle.
- Next row: K.
- Next row: K2, P to end.
- Rep last 2 rows twice more.
- Next row: K.
- Next row: Cast (bind) off 2 sts kwise, P4 [5 sts on needle, including rem st from casting (binding) off], then P 12 sts on needle and then 5 sts on holder. [22 sts]
- K 6 rows.
- Cast (bind) off.

SLEEVES
Make 2
- Cast on 12 sts in coral.
- K 4 rows.
- Work 15 rows in st st beg with a P row.
- Cast (bind) off loosely.

MAKING UP
Seam the coat together as described on page 17 and sew on three buttons.

HAT
- Cast on 30 sts in coral.
- Work 2 rows in st st beg with a K row.
- Next row: Cast (bind) off 12 sts, K to last 12 sts, cast (bind) off last 12 sts.
- Break yarn and with ws facing you, join yarn to rem 6 sts.
- Next row: P.
- Next row: K1, m1, K to last 2 sts, m1, K1. [8 sts]
- Next row: P.
- Rep last 2 rows once more. [10 sts]
- Work 2 rows in st st beg with a K row.
- Next row: K1, ssk, K to last 3 sts, k2tog, K1. [8 sts]
- Next row: P.
- Next row: K1, ssk, K to last 3 sts, k2tog, K1. [6 sts]
- Cast (bind) off pwise.
- With rs of top part of hat facing you, pick up and K 30 sts along cast-on edge.
- Next row: P.
- Next row: K1, (inc1, K1) 28 times, K1. [58 sts]
- Work 6 rows in st st beg with a P row.
- Next row: K.
- Cast (bind) off loosely.

MAKING UP
Join the back seam of the hat and oversew the top part of the hat to the side band. Sew the feathers in place on the front.

SHOES
The shoes are knitted from the top edge to the bottom edge.
Make 2

- Using size 2.25 mm (US 1) needles, cast on 24 sts in burgundy silk rayon embroidery thread.
- Work 5 rows in st st beg with a K row.
- Next row: K.
- Cast (bind) off.

MAKING UP
Fold the strip widthways so that the right sides are together. Oversew the short edge and bottom seam (cast-off edge). Oversew just under 1 cm (³⁄₈ inch) of the top seam (cast-on) edge to form the toe section. Turn the shoe the right way out.

BAG
The bag is knitted as one piece, from the top of the its opening to the tip of the flap.
- Cast on 9 sts in leaf green.
- Work 4 rows in st st beg with a K row.
- Next row: K1, m1, K7, m1, K1. [11 sts]
- Work 5 rows in st st beg with a P row.
- Next row: K1, ssk, K5, k2tog, K1. [9 sts]
- Work 5 rows in st st beg with a P row.
- Next row: K1, ssk, K3, k2tog, K1. [7 sts]
- Next row: P.
- Next row: K1, ssk, K1, k2tog, K1. [5 sts]
- Cast (bind) off kwise.

For the strap, make a 10-cm (4-inch) crochet chain in leaf green.

MAKING UP
Fold the cast-on edge upwards so that it is level with what will be the top of the bag and the right sides of the bag are together. Oversew the side seams and turn the right way out. Fasten the ends of the strap to the sides of the bag, securing the 'tails' in the inside seams. Sew a green button on the top flap of the bag.

To finish, double the bracelet and put it round the doll's neck. Fasten the small rose on the doll's right-hand lapel.

Corgi

You will need

FOR THE DOG
10 g (¼ oz), approx. 10 m/11 yds, of ochre DK yarn
Small amount of cream DK yarn
Very small amounts of black and purple DK yarn
A small star-shaped purple button for the collar
5 g (⅛ oz) polyester toy stuffing

❧

Use size 3 mm (US 2 or 3) knitting needles throughout, unless stated otherwise, and a size 3.25 mm (US D-3) crochet hook

The Queen has owned Pembroke Welsh corgis since she was given her first pet, named Susan, for her eighteenth birthday in 1944. The breed is well known for being hardworking – though if the truth be told, the Queen's own corgis have not had to work that hard. They live in wicker baskets in a box room in the palace and are fed from silver bowls. They are used to journeys in chauffeur-driven limousines and private planes.

BODY & HEAD

SIDE 1
- Cast on 15 sts in ochre.
- Next row: K2, inc1, K6 then turn, leaving rem sts on needle.
- Work on 10 sts just knitted only.
- Next row: P to end.
- Next row: K2, m1, K8 then turn, leaving rem sts on needle.
- Work on 11 sts just knitted only.
- Next row: P.
- Next row: K2, m1, K to end (across all sts on needle). [18 sts]
- Next row: P.
- Next row: K2, m1, K to end. [19 sts]
- Work 3 rows in st st beg with a P row.
- Next row: K17, k2tog. [18 sts]
- Next row: Cast (bind) off 10 sts pwise, P to end. [8 sts]
- Next row: Cast on 5 sts, K to end. [13 sts]
- Next row: p2tog, P to end. [12 sts]
- Next row: K.
- Next row: p2tog, P to end. [11 sts]
- Next row: Cast (bind) off 2 sts, K to end. [9 sts]
- Next row: p2tog, P to end. [8 sts]
- Next row: k2tog, K to end. [7 sts]
- Next row: p2tog, P to end. [6 sts]
- Next row: K.
- Next row: p2tog, P to end. [5 sts]
- Cast (bind) off.

SIDE 2
- Cast on 15 sts in ochre.
- 1st row: P2, inc1 pwise, K6 then turn, leaving rem sts on needle.
- Work on 10 sts just knitted only.
- Next row: K to end.
- Next row: P2, m1 pwise, P8 then turn, leaving rem sts on needle.
- Work on 11 sts just knitted only.
- Next row: K.
- Next row: P2, m1 pwise, P to end (across all sts on needle). [18 sts]

- Next row: K.
- Next row: P2, m1 pwise, P to end. [19 sts]
- Work 3 rows in st st beg with a K row.
- Next row: P17, p2tog. [18 sts]
- Next row: Cast (bind) off 10 sts, K to end. [8 sts]
- Next row: Cast on 5 sts, P to end. [13 sts]
- Next row: k2tog, K to end. [12 sts]
- Next row: P.
- Next row: k2tog, K to end. [11 sts]
- Next row: Cast off 2 sts pwise, P to end. [9 sts]
- Next row: k2tog, K to end. [8 sts]
- Next row: p2tog, P to end. [7 sts]
- Next row: k2tog, K to end. [6 sts]
- Next row: P.
- Next row: k2tog, K to end. [5 sts]
- Cast (bind) off pwise.

FRONT BIB
The bib is knitted from the bottom to the top.
Make 1
- Cast on 4 sts in cream.
- Work 2 rows in st st beg with a K row.
- Next row: K1, m1, K2, m1, K1. [6 sts]
- Next row: P.
- Next row: K1, m1, K4, m1, K1. [8 sts]
- Work 9 rows in st st beg with a P row.
- Cast (bind) off loosely.

BACK LEGS
Make 2
- Cast on 6 sts in cream.
- Work 2 rows in st st beg with a K row.
- Break yarn and join ochre yarn.
- Work 2 rows in st st beg with a K row.
- Next row: K1, m1, K4, m1, K1. [8 sts]
- Next row: P.
- Next row: K1, m1, K6, m1, K1. [10 sts]
- Next row: P.
- Cast (bind) off.

FRONT LEGS
Make 2
- Cast on 6 sts in cream.
- Work 2 rows in st st beg with a K row.
- Cast (bind) off.

EARS
Make 2
- Using size 2.75 mm (US 2) needles, cast on 4 sts in ochre.
- K 3 rows.
- Next row: (k2tog) twice. [2 sts]
- Next row: k2tog.
- Break yarn and pull it through rem st.

COLLAR
Work a 6.5-cm (2½-inch) crochet chain in purple DK yarn.

MAKING UP
Sew the two body and head sides together, leaving a small gap for stuffing. Stuff the dog and close the gap. Seam and stuff the legs and oversew them in position. Oversew the ears in position. Oversew the bib to the front of the dog.

Using black yarn, work a small circle of chain stitch for the nose and two French knots for the eyes. To stop the French knots disappearing or looking uneven, you may want to work a ring of small chain stitches round the eyes using ochre yarn.

Work a row of cream chain stitch round the nose, then down to the top of the bib. Work a row of chain stitch from the top of the nose up the centre of the face and half way back down the face. Separate a short length of black yarn lengthwise so you have two thinner lengths of yarn. Use one of these to make a single straight stitch for the mouth.

Place the collar round the dog's neck and join the two short ends. Stitch the star button in place.

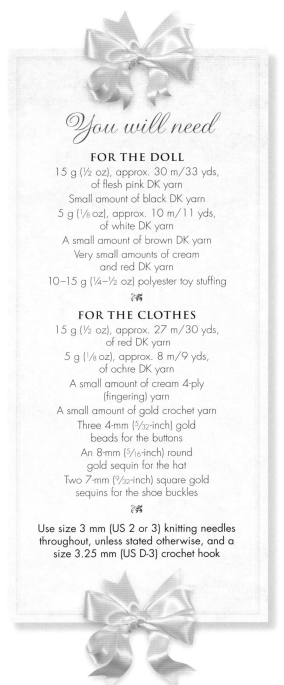

You will need

FOR THE DOLL

15 g (½ oz), approx. 30 m/33 yds,
of flesh pink DK yarn

Small amount of black DK yarn

5 g (⅛ oz), approx. 10 m/11 yds,
of white DK yarn

A small amount of brown DK yarn

Very small amounts of cream
and red DK yarn

10–15 g (¼–½ oz) polyester toy stuffing

FOR THE CLOTHES

15 g (½ oz), approx. 27 m/30 yds,
of red DK yarn

5 g (⅛ oz), approx. 8 m/9 yds,
of ochre DK yarn

A small amount of cream 4-ply
(fingering) yarn

A small amount of gold crochet yarn

Three 4-mm (5/32-inch) gold
beads for the buttons

An 8-mm (5/16-inch) round
gold sequin for the hat

Two 7-mm (9/32-inch) square gold
sequins for the shoe buckles

Use size 3 mm (US 2 or 3) knitting needles
throughout, unless stated otherwise, and a
size 3.25 mm (US D-3) crochet hook

Footman

One of this footman's jobs is to ride on the back of the carriage that takes Prince William and his new bride from Westminster Abbey to the wedding reception at Buckingham Palace. His cheery red and gold outfit with shiny buttons and his quirky hat follow a tradition stretching back hundreds of years.

DOLL

HEAD

The head is knitted from the chin up to the forehead.

Make 2 pieces

- Cast on 10 sts in flesh pink.
- Work 2 rows in st st beg with a K row.
- Next row: K1, m1, K8, m1, K1. [12 sts]
- Work 17 rows in st st beg with a P row.
- Cast (bind) off.

EARS

Make 2

- Cast on 4 sts in flesh pink.
- 1st row: (k2tog) twice. [2 sts]
- Next row: p2tog.
- Break yarn and pull it through rem st.

BODY

The body is worked from the lower edge to the shoulder edge.

Make 2 pieces

- Cast on 14 sts in flesh pink.
- Work 18 rows in st st beg with a K row.
- Next row: Cast (bind) off 1 st, K to end. [13 sts]
- Next row: Cast (bind) off 1 st pwise, P to end. [12 sts]
- Cast (bind) off.

LEGS & SHOES

The legs and shoes are knitted as one piece, from the sole of the shoe to the top of the thigh.

Make 2

- Cast on 28 sts in black.
- Work 4 rows in st st beg with a K row.
- Next row: K6, cast (bind) off 16 sts, K to end. [12 sts]
- Next row: P.
- Break yarn and join white yarn.
- Work 24 rows in st st beg with a K row.
- Cast (bind) off loosely.

ARMS

The arms are knitted from the top of the shoulder to the tip of the hand.

Make 2

- Cast on 9 sts in flesh pink.
- Work 24 rows in st st beg with a K row.
- Next row: K2, k2tog, K1, ssk, K2. [7 sts]
- Next row: p2tog, P3, p2tog. [5 sts]
- Cast (bind) off loosely.

MAKING UP

Stitch the doll together as described on page 16.

FEATURES

Embroider the nose in chain stitch using flesh pink yarn. Using black yarn, embroider two French knots for the eyes.

Using cream yarn, work a ring of chain stitch round each French knot. Separate a short length of red yarn lengthwise so you have two thinner lengths of yarn. Use one length to work a straight stitch for the mouth. Use a red colouring pencil to colour the cheeks.

HAIR

Using brown yarn, embroider three rows of chain stitch for the footman's hair.

BREECHES

The breeches are knitted as one piece.

Make 1

- Cast on 14 sts for first leg in red.
- K 4 rows.
- Work 11 rows in st st beg with a P row.
- Break yarn and leave sts on spare needle.
- Work a second leg exactly as the first but don't break yarn.
- Next row: K 14 sts from second leg then knit across 14 sts from first leg. [28 sts]
- Work 9 rows in st st beg with a P row.
- Next row: (K1, P1) to end.
- Rep last row once more.
- Cast (bind) off quite loosely, keeping to the K1, P1 pattern.

MAKING UP

Seam the breeches together as described on page 17.

COAT

The two front sides and the back of the coat are knitted as one piece, from the lower edge to the neck edge.

Make 1

- Cast on 28 sts in ochre.
- K 2 rows.
- Next row: P.
- Break yarn and join red yarn.

- Work 8 rows in st st beg with a K row.
- Next row: K5, k2tog, K14, ssk, K5. [26 sts]
- Work 3 rows in st st beg with a P row.
- Next row: K5, m1, K16, m1, K5. [28 sts]
- Work 5 rows in st st beg with a P row.
- Next row: K7, turn and work on these sts only, leaving rem sts on needle.
- Work 6 rows in st st beg with a P row. Break yarn.
- With rs facing you, join yarn to rem sts on needle.
- Next row: K14, turn and work on these sts only.
- Work 6 rows in st st beg with a P row.
- Break yarn and leave sts on needle.
- With rs facing you, join yarn to rem 7 sts.
- Work 7 rows in st st beg with a K row.
- Break yarn and join ochre yarn.
- Now work across all 28 sts on needle.
- Next row: p2tog, P7, (p2tog) twice, P2, (p2tog) twice, P to last 2 sts, p2tog. [22 sts]
- K 2 rows.
- Cast (bind) off kwise.
- To make the front edges of the coat, with rs facing you, pick up and K 24 sts along one front edge using ochre yarn.
- K 2 rows.
- Cast (bind) off kwise.
- Work the other front edge in the same way.

SLEEVES

Make 2

- Cast on 12 sts in ochre.
- K 2 rows.
- Break yarn and join red yarn.
- Work 5 rows in st st beg with a P row.
- Break yarn and join ochre yarn.
- Work 2 rows in st st beg with a K row.
- Join red yarn (but do not break ochre yarn).

- Work 4 rows in st st beg with a K row.
- Rep last 6 rows once more.
- Work 2 rows in st st in ochre yarn beg with a K row.
- Work 2 rows in st st in red yarn beg with a K row.
- Cast (bind) off loosely.

MAKING UP

Join the jacket pieces together as described on page 17.

Sew three gold beads onto the left front edge of the footman's coat. The gaps between the stitches on the right front edge will form the buttonholes.

RUFFLE

- Using size 2.25 mm (US 1) needles, cast on 3 sts in cream 4-ply (fingering) yarn.
- 1st row: inc1 into next 2 sts, K1. [5 sts]
- Next row: P.
- Next row: K1, m1, K3, m1, K1. [7 sts]
- K 2 rows.
- Work 3 rows in st st beg with a P row.
- Next row: K1, m1, K5, m1, K1. [9 sts]
- K 2 rows.
- Work 3 rows in st st beg with a P row.
- Next row: K1, m1, K7, m1, K1. [11 sts]
- K 2 rows.
- Work 2 rows in st st beg with a P row.
- Cast (bind) off kwise.

Using the yarn tails, fasten the ruffle round the footman's neck.

HAT

Make 2 pieces
- Cast on 24 sts in black.
- 1st row: K.
- Next row: s1, k1, psso, cast (bind) off 1 st, K to end. [22 sts]
- Next row: s1pwise, P1, psso, cast (bind) off 1 st pwise, P to end. [20 sts]
- Rep last 2 rows twice more. [12 sts]
- Work 6 rows in st st beg with a K row.
- Cast (bind) off.

MAKING UP

Place the two hat pieces right sides together and oversew round the top and 2 cm (¾ inch) along the lower edge.

DECORATION

Turn hat the right way out. Embroider two rows of chain stitch along the sides of the front of the hat using gold crochet yarn. Using the same thread, embroider two short vertical rows of chain stitch at the front of the hat. Fasten the round gold sequin to the front of the hat. Using red DK yarn, make a 12-cm (4½-inch) crochet chain and stitch it round the top edge of the hat.

GLOVES

Make 2
- Using size 2.25 mm (US 1) needles, cast on 11 sts in cream 4-ply (fingering) yarn.
- Work 9 rows in st st beg with a P row.
- Next row: K1, ssk, K5, k2tog, K1. [9 sts]
- Next row: p2tog, P5, p2tog. [7 sts]
- Cast (bind) off.

With right sides together, oversew the glove seams then turn the right way out.

To finish, using black DK yarn, fasten the two square sequins to the shoes as buckles, securing them with a French knot at the top.

Suits

Many gentlemen guests at the wedding will wear a morning suit – a long jacket and striped trousers – plus a top hat. Others will wear an ordinary suit, often called a lounge suit. Eccentric guests may want something different from the traditional colours shown here – so get your fashion design head on and get creative.

You will need

MORNING SUIT, TOP HAT, WAISTCOAT & SHIRT

15 g (½ oz), approx. 31 m/34 yds, of black DK yarn

15 g (½ oz), approx. 18 m/20 yds, of pale grey DK yarn

10 g (¼ oz), approx. 8 m/9 yds, of dark grey DK yarn

A small amount of cream DK yarn

A small amount of white 4-ply (fingering) yarn

A small black button for the jacket

Two 4-mm (5/32-inch) gold beads for the waistcoat buttons

A short length of 7-mm (9/32-inch) wide black ribbon for the hatband

A short length of 1-cm (3/8-inch) wide pale blue/grey ribbon for the tie

LOUNGE SUIT

30 g (1 oz), approx. 42 m/46 yds, of dark grey DK yarn

Two tiny grey buttons for the jacket

Two small snap fasteners for the jacket

Use size 3 mm (US 2 or 3) knitting needles throughout unless stated otherwise

MORNING SUIT JACKET

The two front sides and the back of the jacket are knitted as one piece, from the lower edge to the neck edge.
Make 1

- Cast on 12 sts in black.
- 1st row: K1, inc1, K to last 2 sts, inc1, K to end. [14 sts]
- Next row: K1, inc1, P to last 2 sts, inc1, K to end. [16 sts]
- Rep last 2 rows four times more. [32 sts]
- Next row: K.
- Next row: K2, P to last 2 sts, K2.
- Rep last 2 rows eight times more.
- Next row: K10, turn and work on these sts only, leaving rem sts on needle.
- Next row: P to last 2 sts, K2.
- Next row: K.
- Rep last 2 rows once more.
- Next row: P to last 2 sts, K2.
- Next row: Cast (bind) off 3 sts, K to end. [7 sts]
- Break yarn and leave sts on needle.
- With rs facing you, join yarn to rem 22 sts on needle.
- Next row: K12, turn and work on these sts only, leaving rem sts on needle.
- Work 6 rows in st st beg with a P row.
- Break yarn and leave sts on needle.
- With rs facing you, join yarn to rem 10 sts.
- Next row: K.
- Next row: K2, P to end.
- Rep last 2 rows twice more.
- Next row: K.
- Now work across all sts on needle.
- Next row: Cast (bind) off 3 sts kwise, P6 [7 sts on needle, including rem st from casting off], (p2tog) 6 times, P7. [20 sts]
- K 3 rows.
- Cast (bind) off kwise.

SLEEVES
Make 2
- Cast on 12 sts in black.

- Work 27 rows in st st beg with a P row.
- Cast (bind) off loosely.

MAKING UP
Join the jacket pieces together as described on page 17. Sew the small button to the right-hand side of the jacket.

MORNING SUIT TROUSERS

The trousers are knitted from one side outer edge to the other and as one piece. The normal reverse side is used for the right side.
Make 1

- Cast on 30 sts in dark grey.
- Work 2 rows in st st beg with a K row.
- Join pale grey yarn.
- K 2 rows.
- Rep last 4 rows four times more.
- Using dark grey, work 2 rows in st st beg with a K row.
- Next row: Using pale grey, K.
- Next row: Using pale grey, cast (bind) off 21 sts, K to end. [9 sts]
- Next row: Using dark grey, K.
- Next row: Using dark grey, cast on 21 sts, P to end. [30 sts]
- Using pale grey K 2 rows.
- Using dark grey, work 2 rows in st st beg with a K row.
- Rep last 4 rows four times more.
- Next row: Using pale grey, K.
- Cast (bind) off.
- With the reverse side facing you (this is the right side of the trousers) and using dark grey, pick up and K 28 sts along top edge of the trousers.
- Next row: (K1, P1) to end.
- Rep last row once more.
- Cast (bind) off keeping to the K1, P1 pattern.

MAKING UP
Seam the trousers together as described on page 17.

WAISTCOAT
Make 1

- Cast on 22 sts in cream.
- 1st row: K1, P to last st, K1.
- Next row: K1, inc1, K to last 2 sts, inc1, K to end. [24 sts]
- Next and every ws row: K1, P to last st, K1.
- Rep last 2 rows twice more. [28 sts]
- Work 6 rows as set.
- Next row: K8, turn and work on these sts only, leaving rem sts on needle.
- Next row: K1, P to last st, K1.
- Next row: K1, k2tog, K to end. [7 sts]
- Next row: K1, P to last st, K1.
- Rep last 2 rows three times more. [4 sts]
- Next row: K.
- Break yarn and leave sts on needle.
- With rs facing you, join yarn to rem 20 sts on needle.
- Next row: K12, turn and work on these sts only, leaving rem sts on needle.
- Next row: K1, P to last st, K1.
- Rep last 2 rows once more.
- Next row: K1, k2tog, K to last 3 sts, ssk, K1. [10 sts]
- Next row: K1, P to last st, K1.
- Rep last 2 rows once more. [8 sts]
- Next row: K.
- Next row: K1, P to last st, K1.
- Next row: K.
- Break yarn and leave sts on needle.
- With rs facing you, join yarn to rem 8 sts.
- Next row: K.
- Next row: K1, P to last st, K1.
- Next row: K to last 3 sts, ssk, K1. [7 sts]
- Next row: K1, P to last st, K1.
- Rep last 2 rows three times more. [4 sts]
- Next row: K.
- Now work across all sts on needle.
- Next row: K. [16 sts]
- Cast (bind) off.

MAKING UP
Sew the gold beads onto one edge.

SHIRT

Make 1

- Using size 2.25 mm (US 1) needles, cast on 16 sts in white 4-ply (fingering) yarn.
- Work 16 rows in st st beg with a K row.
- Next row: K3, loosely cast off 10 sts, K to end. [6 sts]
- Next row: P3, cast on 10 sts, P3. [16 sts]
- Work 16 rows in st st beg with a K row.
- Cast (bind) off.
- For the collar, using size 2.25 mm (US 1) needles, cast on 38 sts in white 4-ply (fingering) yarn.
- Work 5 rows in st st beg with a K row.
- Cast (bind) off kwise.

MAKING UP

Oversew the collar to top of shirt so that two short edges form the front of the collar. Tie the ribbon round the neck in a standard tie knot.

TOP HAT

Make 1

- Cast on 30 sts in pale grey.
- Work 11 rows in st st beg with a K row.
- Next row: Cast off 12 sts kwise, P5 [6 sts on needle, including rem st from casting off], cast off 12 sts kwise. [6 sts]
- Break yarn and rejoin yarn to rs of work.
- Next row: K1, m1, K to last 2 sts, m1, K1. [8 sts]
- Next row: P.
- Rep last 2 rows twice more. [12 sts]
- Next row: K1, ssk, K to last 3 sts, k2tog, K1. [10 sts]
- Next row: P.
- Rep last 2 rows once more. [8 sts]
- Next row: K1, ssk, K2, k2tog, K1. [6 sts]
- Cast (bind) off pwise.
- With rs facing you, pick up and knit 30 sts along cast-on edge.
- Next row: P.

- Next row: K1, (inc1, K1) 28 times, K1. [58 sts]
- Next row: P.
- Cast (bind) off.

MAKING UP

To make up, join the back seam of the hat and oversew the top part of the hat to the sides. Wrap the ribbon round the hat and sew or glue the ends together at the back.

LOUNGE SUIT JACKET

The two front sides and the back of the jacket are knitted as one piece, from the lower edge to the neck edge.
Make 1

- Cast on 36 sts in dark grey.
- 1st row: K2, P to last 2 sts, K2.
- Next row: K.
- Rep last 2 rows seven times more.
- Next row: K2, P to last 2 sts, K2.
- Next row: K11, turn and work on these sts only, leaving rem sts on needle.
- Next row: P to last 2 sts, K2.
- Next row: K.
- Rep last 2 rows once more.
- Next row: P to last 2 sts, K2.
- Next row: Cast (bind) off 3 sts, K to end. [8 sts]
- Break yarn and leave sts on needle.
- With rs facing you, join yarn to rem 25 sts on needle.
- Next row: K14, turn and work on these sts only, leaving rem sts on needle.
- Work 6 rows in st st beg with a P row.
- Break yarn and leave sts on needle.
- With rs facing you, join yarn to rem 11 sts.
- Next row: K.
- Next row: K2, P to end.
- Rep last 2 rows once more.
- Next row: K.
- Now work across all sts on needle.
- Next row: Cast (bind) off 3 sts kwise,

P7 [8 sts on needle, including rem st from casting off], (p2tog) 3 times, P2, (p2tog) 3 times, P8. [24 sts]
- K 3 rows.
- Cast (bind) off.

SLEEVES

Make 2

- Cast on 12 sts in dark grey.
- K 2 rows.
- Work 23 rows in st st beg with a P row.
- Cast (bind) off loosely.

MAKING UP

Join the jacket pieces together as described on page 17. Sew two small buttons to the left-hand side of the jacket. Sew the top part of the snap fastener underneath the buttons and the lower part on the top of the right-hand side edge.

LOUNGE SUIT TROUSERS

The trousers are knitted as one piece.
Make 1

- Cast on 14 sts for the first leg in dark grey.
- K 2 rows.
- Work 27 rows in st st beg with a P row.
- Break yarn and leave sts on a spare needle or stitch holder.
- Work a second trouser leg exactly as the first but don't break yarn.
- Next row: K 14 sts from second trouser leg then knit across 14 sts from first trouser leg. [28 sts]
- Work 9 rows in st st beg with a P row.
- Next row: (K1, P1) to end.
- Rep last row once more.
- Cast (bind) off quite loosely, keeping to the K1, P1 pattern.

MAKING UP

Seam the trousers together as described on page 17.

Dresses & Hats

Here we present a range of outfits for the female wedding guests. Sit down with your knitting stash, choose your favourite colours and combinations and start knitting your own selection.

You will need

PURPLE DRESS
10 g (¼ oz), approx. 16 m/17 yds, purple DK yarn
A small flower-shaped pale pink button

LIME GREEN DRESS
15 g (½ oz), approx. 26 m/28 yds, lime green DK yarn
A ready-made ribbon bow

PINK CARDIGAN
10 g (¼ oz), approx. 23 m/25 yds, mid-pink DK yarn
Two tiny purple buttons

TEAL CAPELET
10 g (¼ oz), approx. 13 m/14 yds, teal DK yarn
A small button

MAUVE BERET
5 g (⅛ oz), approx. 7 m/8 yds,
of pale mauve DK yarn
A ready-made ribbon bow

TURQUOISE HAT
10 g (¼ oz), approx. 16 m/17 yds, turquoise DK yarn
A small length of cream ribbon
A ready-made ribbon flower

PINK HAT
5 g (⅛ oz), approx. 11 m/12 yds,
of pastel pink DK yarn
A ready-made ribbon bow
A ready-made ribbon rose

CATHERINE'S BLUE DRESS
20 g (¾ oz), approx. 24 m/26 yds, bright blue DK yarn

Use size 3 mm (US 2 or 3) knitting needles
and a size 3.25 mm (US D-3) crochet hook

PURPLE DRESS

The front and back of the dress are identical.
Make 2 pieces

- Cast on 20 sts in purple.
- Work 3 rows in st st beg with a P row.
- Next row: K2, k2tog, K to last 4 sts, ssk, K2. [18 sts]
- K 2 rows.
- Next row: P.
- Rep last 4 rows twice more. [14 sts]
- Next row: K2, k2tog, K to last 4 sts, ssk, K2. [12 sts]
- Next row: K.
- Work 3 rows in st st beg with a K row.
- Next row: K.
- Work 4 rows in st st beg with a K row.
- Next row: K2, m1, K8, m1, K2. [14 sts]
- Next row: P.
- Next row: K2, m1, K10, m1, K2. [16 sts]
- Work 3 rows in st st beg with a P row.
- Next row: k2tog, K3, cast off 6 sts, K to last 2 sts, ssk.
- Turn and cont on last 4 sts only, leaving rem sts on the needle.
- Next row: p2tog, P2. [3 sts]
- Next row: K.
- Next row: P.
- Next row: k2tog, K1. [2 sts]
- Next row: P.
- Next row: k2tog, break yarn and pull tail through rem st.
- With ws facing you, join yarn to rem 4 sts.
- Next row: P2, p2tog. [3 sts]
- Next row: K.
- Next row: P.
- Next row: K1, k2tog. [2 sts]
- Next row: P.
- Next row: k2tog, break yarn and pull tail through rem st.

MAKING UP

Seam the dress together as described on page 17. Sew the flower-shaped pale pink button in place.

LIME GREEN DRESS

The front and back of the dress are identical.
Make 2 pieces

- Cast on 48 sts in lime green.
- Work 7 rows in st st beg with a P row.
- Next row: (s1, k2tog, psso) 16 times. [16 sts]
- Next row: K.
- Work 6 rows in st st beg with a K row.
- Next row: K2, k2tog, K to last 4 sts, ssk, K2. [14 sts]
- Work 3 rows in st st beg with a P row.
- Rep last 4 rows once more. [12 sts]
- Work 2 rows in st st beg with a K row.
- Next row: K2, m1, K8, m1, K2. [14 sts]
- Next row: P.
- Next row: K2, m1, K10, m1, K2. [16 sts]
- Work 3 rows in st st beg with a P row.
- Next row: k2tog, K6, turn and cont on last 7 sts only, leaving other sts on the needle.
- Next row: P.
- Next row: K5, ssk. [6 sts]
- Next row: P.
- Next row: k2tog, K2, ssk. [4 sts]
- Next row: (p2tog) twice. [2 sts]
- Next row: k2tog, break yarn and pull tail through rem st.
- With rs facing you, join yarn to rem sts.
- Next row: K6, ssk. [7 sts]
- Next row: P.
- Next row: k2tog, K5. [6 sts]
- Next row: P.
- Next row: k2tog, K2, ssk. [4 sts]
- Next row: (p2tog) twice. [2 sts]
- Next row: k2tog, break yarn and pull tail through rem st.

MAKING UP

Seam the dress together as described on page 17. Sew the ribbon bow in place.

PINK CARDIGAN

The two front sides and the back of the cardigan are knitted as one piece.
Make 1

- Cast on 36 sts in mid-pink.
- 1st row: K2, P to last 2 sts, K2.
- Next row: K.
- Next row: K2, P to last 2 sts, K2.
- Next row: K8, ssk, K16, k2tog, K8. [34 sts]
- Next and every ws row: K2, P to last 2 sts, K2.
- Work 2 rows as set.
- Next row: K7, ssk, k2tog, K12, ssk, k2tog, K7. [30 sts]
- Work 3 rows as set.
- Next row: K8, turn and work on these sts only, leaving rem sts on needle.
- Next row: P to last 2 sts, K2.
- Next row: K.
- Rep last 2 rows twice more.
- Break yarn and leave sts on needle.
- With rs facing you, join yarn to rem 22 sts on needle.
- Next row: K14, turn and work on these sts only, leaving rem sts on needle.
- Work 6 rows in st st beg with a P row.
- Break yarn and leave rem sts on needle.
- With rs facing you, join yarn to rem 8 sts on needle.
- Next row: K.
- Next row: K2, P to end.
- Rep last 2 rows twice more.
- Next row: K.
- Now work across all 30 sts on needle.
- Next row: k2tog, K4, k2tog, K1, (k2tog) 3 times, (ssk) 3 times, K1, ssk, K4, ssk. [20 sts]
- K 7 rows.
- Cast (bind) off.

SLEEVES
Make 2
- Cast on 14 sts in mid-pink.
- K 2 rows.
- Work 15 rows in st st beg with a P row.
- Cast (bind) off.

MAKING UP
Seam the cardigan together as described on page 17. Sew the two small buttons on the left-hand side of the cardigan. The gaps between stitches on the right-hand side can be used for buttonholes

TEAL CAPELET
The cape is knitted as one piece, from the neck edge to the lower edge.
Make 1
- Cast on 24 sts in teal, leaving a long tail of yarn for making the button loop for the cape.
- K 2 rows.
- Next row: K5, inc1 into next 2 sts, K10, inc1 into next 2 sts, K5. [28 sts]
- Next and every ws row: K2, P to last 2 sts, K2.
- Next rs row: K6, inc1 into next 2 sts, K12, inc1 into next 2 sts, K6. [32 sts]
- Next rs row: K7, inc1 into next 2 sts, K14, inc1 into next 2 sts, K7. [36 sts]

- Next rs row: K8, inc1 into next 2 sts, K16, inc1 into next 2 sts, K8. [40 sts]
- Next rs row: K9, inc1 into next 2 sts, K18, inc1 into next 2 sts, K9. [44 sts]
- Next rs row: K10, inc1 into next 2 sts, K20, inc1 into next 2 sts, K10. [48 sts]
- Next row: K2, P to last 2 sts, K2.
- Next row: K1, (yfwd, k2tog) 23 times, K1.
- Next row: K2, P to last 2 sts, K2.
- K 2 rows.
- Cast (bind) off kwise loosely.

MAKING UP
Use the tail at the neck edge to work a 1-cm (3/8-inch) crochet chain and sew the end in place to create a button loop. Sew the button onto the opposite side of the capelet.

MAUVE BERET
Make 1
- Cast on 22 sts in mauve.
- K 2 rows.
- Next row: P.
- Next row: K1, (m1, K1) to end. [43 sts]
- K 2 rows.
- Next row: Cast (bind) off 18 sts, K7 [including rem st from casting off], cast (bind) off 18 sts. [7 sts]
- Break yarn and rejoin to rs of rem 7 sts.
- Next row: K1, m1, K to last st, m1, K1. [9 sts]
- Next row: P.
- Rep last 2 rows four times more. [17 sts]
- Next row: K1, k2tog, K to last 3 sts, ssk, K1. [15 sts]

- Next row: P.
- Rep last 2 rows three times more. [9 sts]
- Next row: K1, k2tog, K3, ssk, K1. [7 sts]
- Cast (bind) off pwise.

MAKING UP
Join the back seam of the beret and oversew the top part of the hat to the sides. Sew the ribbon bow in place.

TURQUOISE HAT
Make 1
- Cast on 30 sts in turquoise.
- Work 4 rows in st st beg with a K row.
- Next row: Cast off 12 sts, K6 [including rem st from casting off], cast (bind) off 12 sts. [6 sts]
- Break yarn and rejoin to rs of rem 6 sts.
- Next row: P.
- Next row: K1, m1, K to last 2 sts, m1, K1. [8 sts]
- Next row: P.
- Rep last 2 rows once more. [10 sts]
- Work 2 rows in st st beg with a K row.
- Next row: K1, ssk, K4, k2tog, K1. [8 sts]
- Next row: P.
- Next row: K1, ssk, K2, k2tog, K1. [6 sts]
- Cast (bind) off pwise.
- With rs facing, pick up and K 30 sts along cast-on edge.

- Next row: P.
- Next row: K1, inc1 into next 28 sts, K1. [58 sts]
- Next row: P.
- K 3 rows.
- Rep last 4 rows once more.
- Next row: P.
- Cast (bind) off.

MAKING UP

Join the back seam of the hat and oversew the top part of the hat to the side band. Sew the flower to the middle of the ribbon. Wrap the ribbon round the hat and sew or glue the ends together.

PINK HAT

Make 1

- Cast on 46 sts in pastel pink.
- Work 3 rows in st st beg with a P row.
- Next row: (K1, s1, K1, psso) 15 times. [31 sts]
- Work 11 rows in st st beg with a P row.
- Next row: Cast (bind) off 12 sts, K7 [including rem st from casting (binding) off], cast off 12 sts.
- Break yarn and rejoin to ws of rem 7 sts.
- Next row: P.
- Next row: K1, m1, K to last 2 sts, m1, K1. [9 sts]
- Next row: P.
- Rep last 2 rows once more. [11 sts]
- Work 2 rows in st st beg with a K row.
- Next row: K1, k2tog, K5, ssk, K1. [9 sts]
- Next row: P.
- Next row: K1, k2tog, K3, ssk, K1. [7 sts]
- Cast (bind) off pwise.

MAKING UP

Join the back seam of the hat and oversew the top part of the hat to the sides. Sew the ribbon bow and ribbon rose in place.

CATHERINE'S BLUE DRESS

This dress is based on the elegant bright blue dress that Kate wore when the royal engagement was announced.

FRONT

- Cast on 20 sts in bright blue.
- Work 3 rows in st st beg with a P row.
- Next row: K1, k2tog, K to last 3 sts, ssk, K1. [18 sts]
- Work 3 rows in st st beg with a P row.
- Rep last 4 rows three times more. [12 sts]
- Work 2 rows in st st beg with a K row.
- Next row: K2, m1, K8, m1, K2. [14 sts]
- Next row: P.
- Next row: K2, m1, K10, m1, K2. [16 sts]
- Work 3 rows in st st beg with a P row.*
- Mark beg and end of last row with a thread or small safety pin.
- Next row: k2tog, K6, turn and cont on last 7 sts only, leaving other sts on the needle.
- Next and every ws row: P.
- Next rs row: K5, ssk. [6 sts]
- Next rs row: K4, ssk. [5 sts]
- Next rs row: K3, ssk. [4 sts]
- Cast (bind) off pwise.
- With rs facing you, join yarn to rem sts.
- Next row: K6, ssk. [7 sts]
- Next and every ws row: P.
- Next rs row: ssk, K5. [6 sts]
- Next rs row: ssk, K4. [5 sts]
- Next rs row: ssk, K3. [4 sts]
- Cast (bind) off pwise.

BACK

Work as for front to *.
- Next row: K1, k2tog, K to last 3 sts, ssk, K1. [14 sts].
- Work 3 rows in st st beg with a P row.
- Next row: K4, cast off 6 sts, K to end.
- Work on last 4 sts only, leaving rem sts on needle.

- Work 2 rows in st st beg with a P row.
- Cast (bind) off pwise.
- Break yarn and rejoin to ws of rem 4 sts.
- Work 2 rows in st st beg with a P row.
- Cast (bind) off pwise.

SLEEVES

Make 2

- Cast on 12 sts.
- Work 21 rows in st st beg with a P row.
- Cast (bind) off loosely.

MAKING UP

Seam the dress together as described on page 17, leaving a 2.5 cm (1 inch) opening at the armhole edges for inserting the sleeves. For the front wrap feature, embroider four lines of chain stitch in a cross shape, using the photograph below as a guide.

Index